Step by Step
to
Stand-Up Comedy

Greg Dean

Foreword by
Steve Allen

HEINEMANN
Portsmouth, NH

Heinemann

361 Hanover Street
Portsmouth, NH 03801–3912
www.heinemanndrama.com

Offices and agents throughout the world

Greg Dean's website can be found at: www.stand-upcomedy.com

Library of Congress Cataloging-in-Publication Data
Dean, Greg.
   Step by step to stand-up comedy / Greg Dean ; foreword by Steve Allen.
     p.   cm.
   ISBN 0–325–00179–0 (pbk. : acid-free paper)
   1. Stand-up comedy. I. Title.

PN1969.C65 D43   2000
792.7'028–dc21   00-039555

Editor: Lisa A. Barnett
Production coordinator: Vicki Kasabian
Production service: Denise Botelho/Colophon
Cover design: Jenny Jensen Greenleaf
Manufacturing: Deanna Richardson

Printed in the United States of America on acid-free paper
11 10   **VP**   **12 13**

For my mother—I can still hear your laughter.

Contents

Foreword

How-to books about comedy are a dime a dozen. I've written two of them myself. But some are better than others—the present volume, for example, by Greg Dean.

A good many of the points on which Dean offers instructions are lessons I had to learn the hard way. I wish books of this sort had been available in those days.

Most of us would never dream of offering professional advice to a TV repairman, a brain surgeon, or a defensive lineman for the Chicago Bears, but we all apparently view ourselves as qualified to offer advice to Eddie Murphy, Jackie Mason, or Dennis Miller.

Greg Dean, by way of contrast, knows the territory he's writing about and provides a wealth of nuts-and-bolts advice about the kinds of stories that audiences will interpret as funny.

STEVE ALLEN

Acknowledgments

I am grateful to so many people for putting up with me and my obsession for modeling the underlying structure of comedy. I know I've driven many people crazy by calling them at all hours of the night with questions, ramblings, and incoherent theories. My favorite aspect of uncovering these techniques has been the long walks and talks with my friends. In particular, I wish to deeply thank my dear friend and co-comedy theorist Frank Miles (who is responsible for some of the techniques and some of the rewriting of this book), Gayla Johnson (the love of my life), Andy Davis (who has been there from the beginning), Bill Fulco (the only one to outwalk and outtalk me), and the members of the Friday Night Movie Group: Bennett I. Goldberg, Jeff Weakley, and Derek Loughran. I'm also grateful for the support of Tim Simpson, Peter Desberg, Jay Douglas, Dan Goldman, David Reskin, Will Patrick, Allan Murray, Rick Patton, Tyrum Dean, Dona Silvers (mom), Michael Davis (it got done), Frank Olivier, and Mark Whalen. I wish to offer a sincere thanks to Judy DeLozier, Phil and Norma Barretta, and Buddha for their inspiration and encouragement. And of course, Ingrid Reese for her sense of rhythm while proofreading and editing. I also want to thank Victor Raskin, whose *Semantic Theory of Humor* (Dordrecht-Boston: D. Reidel, 1985) is the inspirational breakthrough on which much of my comedy model has been based. A special thanks to John Grinder and Richard Bandler for cofounding Neuro-Linguistic Programming (NLP). Without a mental map to make a mental map, my work would not have been possible. I especially acknowledge the contribution of John Grinder, who gave me personal guidance as I was forming this comedy model and the ensuing exercises. On the business end, this book has been much improved with the valuable suggestions of both my agent, Scott Edelstein and my editor, Lisa Barnett. And lastly, but not leastly, I want to thank all of my students for allowing me to learn from them while they were paying me. Thank you all!

Do You Have What It Takes to Be a Comedian?

Are You Funny?

Were you always kept after school for being the class cutup?

Can you do an impression of your boss?

Do people often look at you like the RCA Victor dog?

Do You Need Money?

Are you on a first-name basis with everyone at the unemployment office?

Do you know what's happening on *As the World Turns*?

Have you been considering teaching Driver's Ed.?

Have You Lived a Bizarre Life?

Are you on the outside looking out?

Did you hit your head really hard when you were a kid?

During your first sexual encounter, did you use jumper cables?

Do You Love to Make People Laugh?

Have you ignored all of your teachers' efforts to shut you up since kindergarten?

Have you been fired for doing an impression of your boss?

Are you still using jumper cables?

If you answered yes to any of these questions you might as well admit it: You're one of the addicted. You're a joke-aholic. But you can find help at the Shtick Center for the Chronically Funny.

You may be thinking, "Those professional comedians are great!" They are, but there's no difference between you and them that a little knowledge and experience can't fix. At one time, they were just like you. Like successful people in any other job, they got where they are through hard work. You, however, have the advantage: this indispensable guide, which will take you step-by-step toward a career in stand-up comedy.

So if making a living being funny appeals to you, read on. . . .

1

The Secrets of Joke Structure

What is a joke? Funny you should ask. Most people would define a joke as something someone says or does that makes others laugh. That statement, though true, doesn't really tell us what a joke *is*. It just describes the desired *effect*. What about jokes that get a huge laugh in one situation and a roar of silence in another? If a joke doesn't get a laugh, does it suddenly stop being a joke?

People usually recognize a joke whether it makes them laugh or not. Why? Because there is some consistent, intrinsic *structure* that everyone identifies as a joke. Until now, no one has presented this structure in an understandable manner. That's about to change. Explaining joke structure is exactly what this chapter is all about.

Setup and Punch

Let's begin with what most people already know about jokes. Traditionally, a joke contains two parts: (1) the *setup* and (2) the *punch*. Take this joke, for example, by A. Whitney Brown:

> I saw my grandmother the other day . . . probably for the last time.
> . . . Oh, she's not sick or anything, she just bores the hell out of me.

To help explain joke structure, I've designed a visual device I call the *Joke Diagram*. Let's place the above joke in Diagram 1 so you can clearly identify the setup and punch:

Diagram 1

I saw my grandmother the other day . . . probably for the last time. . . . Oh, she's not sick or anything,

Setup

she just bores the hell out of me.

Punch

The setup and punch are usually defined in this way:

The *setup* is the first part of joke that sets up the laugh.
The *punch* is the second part that makes you laugh.

That's great, except for one small problem: It doesn't really explain anything. Let's see if we can do better.

What a Joke Does:
Expectation and Surprise

The setup and the punch are directly related to *expectation* and *surprise*. Take this joke by Steve Martin; notice how the setup causes you to *expect* something:

Sex is one of the most beautiful, wholesome, and natural things—

Then see how the punch *surprises* you with:

—that money can buy.

At this point you may be thinking, "That's it—expectation and surprise? What's the big deal about that?" Well, the big deal is this: In order to work, a joke *has* to surprise you. The trick is that you cannot be surprised unless you're expecting something else first. That's what a joke does: It causes you to expect one thing, then surprises you with another. So, here's a revised definition:

The Setup creates an expectation.
The Punch reveals a surprise.

2

Now that you understand this, you should be able to write a great joke, right?

Wrong. It isn't enough to know *what* a joke does. You need to know *how* a joke does it.

How a Joke Works:
1st Story and 2nd Story

In an article entitled "Jokes," (*Psychology Today*, October 1985), Victor Raskin offered a "script-based semantic theory of humor," which proposed that a "sentence joke" has two scripts. However, because it's a semantic theory, dealing only with words and their implications, its application to physical and nonverbal comedy was limited. I altered Raskin's term from *script* to *story*, which made it possible for me to apply this concept to all forms of humor, not just language-based jokes. Through Raskin's insight, I found the first piece of joke structure. The evolution of my Joke Diagram began with this discovery.

> **SECRET #1:**
> **A JOKE REQUIRES TWO STORY LINES.**

The setup of a joke creates a *1st story* in our minds that leads us to expect something, then the punch surprises us with a *2nd story* that's compatible with, yet somehow different from, what we're expecting. For example, imagine a male comic, appearing to be completely grief-stricken, telling this joke:

(SADLY) My wife just ran off with my best friend. Boy, do I miss *him*.

The setup creates a 1st story: A man is unhappy because *he misses his wife*. We expect the story to continue along that theme, so we're surprised when the punch reveals a 2nd story: A man is unhappy because *he misses his buddy*.

Putting this joke in Diagram 2 will give you a visual depiction of how the setup and punch create and reveal these two story lines:

Diagram 2

(SADLY) My wife just ran off with my best friend.

Setup	
	1st Story: *He's unhappy because he misses his wife.*
	2nd Story: *He's unhappy because he misses his buddy.* Boy, do I miss *him.*"

Punch

If a joke doesn't have two story lines, *it's not a joke.* So, if the punch doesn't reveal a 2nd story line, then what you've got is a sort of single-story story, but not a joke. For instance:

(SADLY) My wife just ran off with my best friend. Boy, do I miss *her.*

Not exactly a knee-slapper. This starts off as a story about a man missing his wife, and it ends up the same way. There's no 2nd story, so there's no surprise. And since there's no surprise. there's no joke.

Setup and 1st Story

What's the difference between the 1st story and the setup? Actually, these two elements fulfill very different functions within joke structure. As the first part of the joke, the setup is the *words and/or actions used to get the audience to expect something.* Nothing more. Then, based on the setup, the 1st story is the *detailed scene imagined by the audience* of what they expect to be true.

Let me illustrate this with an old standard joke:

For forty years I've been married and in love with the same woman. If my wife ever finds out she'll kill me.

When the comic says, "For forty years I've been married and in love with the same woman," *that*—and only that—is the setup. Then from hearing this setup the audience imagines a much more elaborate 1st story. Since the 1st story is created in the minds of the audience, I can't say *exactly* what it would be for each individual, so here's my version:

This man is bragging about being deeply in love with his wife. In

4

their forty years together, they have built a rich and full life and were able to work out their differences and remain happy. He has never cheated on her and plans to be with her the rest of his life.

That's more or less the 1st story most people would construct. As you can see, the 1st story has considerably more detail than the setup. So where does all that detail come from?

This larger story has been built by making assumptions about the information in the setup. Assumptions allow us to make sense of something when we get limited information. Based on our own life experience, we constantly make this kind of speculative leap. So naturally, the 1st story contains much more information than the setup.

Punch and 2nd Story

The relationship between the punch and the 2nd story parallels that of the setup and the 1st story. As the second part of the joke, the punch is the *words and/or actions used to surprise the audience.* Nothing more. Based on the punch, the audience imagines a detailed 2nd story that is compatible with the setup, yet is unexpected.

Still using the same joke's punch, "If my wife ever finds out she'll kill me," here's my version of the 2nd story:

Despite staying in a terrible marriage, this man has never divorced. To find some happiness, he's fallen in love with a mistress and has been able to work it out with her so she'd stay with him for forty years even though he's remained married. He lives in constant fear that his wife will find out about his long-time affair and make his life with her more miserable than it already is.

Again, the 2nd story is a much more detailed scenario than the punch. You may have imagined a slightly different scene, yet the gist of the story will remain fairly consistent from person to person.

What I want to emphasize is how much information resides within a joke that's *not* stated in the setup or the punch—the information we add by making assumptions.

WHAT EXACTLY IS AN ASSUMPTION?
I'm sorry, I assumed you knew. An assumption can be any thought based on taking something for granted, presupposing, conjecturing, presum-

ing, forecasting, projecting onto, theorizing about, speculating upon, or accepting that something is as it's always been.

> **SECRET #2:**
>
> **EVERY PART OF A THING YOU *IMAGINE* EXISTS—**
> **BUT AREN'T DIRECTLY PERCEIVING—IS AN ASSUMPTION.**

Any aspect of a something you cannot see, hear, feel, taste, or smell exists only as an assumption. The chances are that it does exist, but since you have no direct evidence that it does, you're making an assumption.

We do this because human beings, as a rule, have a profound need for things to make sense. If something doesn't make sense, we'll *fill in* the information so it will make sense, and we do that by making assumptions based on our past experience.

Doing this is not a bad thing. In fact, it's absolutely necessary. Imagine a world without assumptions. You'd have to carefully test each step you took to make sure the floor would hold your weight. You'd have to peek behind everything to find out whether the backs were actually there. You'd have to look in a mirror to make sure you're still human. You'd have to call the IRS every year to determine if they still wanted your money. Get the idea?

The fact that our perspective limits the information we can experience directly, and that we fill in the remaining void with assumptions allows us to be surprised by something other than what we assumed. It's this mental phenomenon that makes jokes possible.

As I've mentioned, the setup and the 1st story and the punch and the 2nd story are different but necessary elements of joke structure. All of these things show how a joke works. So now you know exactly how to write a joke, right?

Well, er, no. Not quite. In order to write a joke, you'll need to know the three mechanisms for constructing and connecting the 1st story and 2nd story.

The Three Mechanisms of Joke Structure

When we examine *how* a joke works, we're looking for the exact mechanisms it uses to achieve its effect. Understanding the mechanisms will soon enable you to use my step-by-step joke-writing system: the Joke Prospector (see Chapter 2).

So far, you've learned that the setup creates a 1st story, which leads to certain expectations, and then the punch reveals an unexpected 2nd story. *How* is this accomplished?

Target Assumption and Reinterpretation: Two Interpretations of One Thing

I call the first two mechanisms of joke structure *target assumption* and *reinterpretation*. These are related mechanisms, with the target assumption the key ingredient of the 1st story and the reinterpretation the pivotal component of the 2nd story. I say "related mechanisms" because each represents a different interpretation of the same thing. The target assumption presents an *expected* interpretation of that thing and the reinterpretation reveals an *unexpected* interpretation of that very same thing.

TARGET ASSUMPTION: JOKES WITH SETUPS

As discussed earlier, when an audience sees or hears a setup they build a 1st story by making a vast number of assumptions. One of these assumptions will be the *target assumption*. What sets the target assumption apart from the other assumptions is that it fulfills two unique criteria.

1. The target assumption is the key assumption upon which the 1st story is built. Of all the assumptions made to imagine a story, one key assumption gives the 1st story its specific meaning. That is, if you don't make that key or target assumption, you'll imagine a very different story than the one required to make the joke work. Take this old joke, for example:

> I had a mud pack facial done, and for three days my face looked much better. Then the mud fell off.

The effectiveness of the setup hinges on your making a target assumption—*that the mud was taken off as part of the facial.* Making that (key) target assumption led you to imagine a 1st story, in which *the mud pack facial gave the comic nicer-looking skin for three days.* Then the punch surprised you by revealing a very different 2nd story—*that the comic walked around for three days with a mud-covered face, which actually improved his or her looks.* Diagram 3 shows where the target assumption fits on the Joke Diagram.

7

Diagram 3

I had a mud pack facial done, and for three days my face looked much better.

Setup

> **1st Story:** *The facial gave the comic nice-looking skin for three days.*
>
> **Target Assumption:** *The mud was taken off as part of the facial.*
>
> **2nd Story:** *The comic walked around for three days with a mud-covered face, which actually improved his or her looks.*
>
> Then the mud fell off.

Punch

2. *The target assumption is the assumption directly shattered by the punch.* Every joke with a setup is designed to manipulate an audience into imagining a 1st story by making assumptions. The punch then reveals a 2nd story that surprises the audience by targeting one key assumption and making it wrong. For instance, of all the assumptions you made about the setup of the above joke, only the target assumption—*the mud was taken off as part of the facial*—was directly shattered by the punch—"Then the mud fell off."

TARGET ASSUMPTION: JOKES WITHOUT SETUPS

You might be asking yourself, "What about all those funny comments I laugh at that don't have setups?" It's a fact that there's a whole class of jokes that have no formal setups. Strangely enough, they still have a target assumption, but there's no need for a setup because the *target assumption already resides in the minds of the audience.*

Let me illustrate this with something that actually happened to me. I was sitting in a Chinese restaurant late one night. It was an authentic establishment, and most of the other patrons were Asian immigrants, many of whom spoke little or no English. They had a TV up in the corner of the room where everyone could see it, and a Gallagher concert was starting.

Gallagher made his entrance riding a bicycle with square wheels, and everybody cracked up laughing. Regardless of language or cultural differences, everyone had the *target assumption* that for a wheel to work properly it must be round. Because this information is universally accepted, there's no need for a setup. For the joke to succeed, all that was needed was a punch—in the form of square wheels—which made this existing target assumption wrong.

Many jokes have target assumptions that most people accept based on physical laws, societal biases, cultural and national presuppositions, accepted definitions, stereotypes, and familiar environments, to name a few examples. On a daily basis, people make millions of assumptions without even realizing it. It's these unconscious assumptions that are targeted by jokes without setups. Whenever anyone assumes anything, you've got the makings of a joke. This is where reinterpretation comes in.

REINTERPRETATION: JOKES WITH PUNCHES

We know that the setup creates an expectation when the audience builds a 1st story by making assumptions; the punch then shatters a key assumption (the target assumption) and reveals a 2nd story. The punch does this by presenting an *unexpected interpretation* of something in the setup. This unexpected interpretation is called *reinterpretation*. The reinterpretation must adhere to two rules, described below.

1. The reinterpretation is the idea upon which the punch's 2nd story is based. Just as the target assumption creates the 1st story, the reinterpretation creates the 2nd story. Take this joke for example:

> My grandfather died peacefully in his sleep. But the kids on his bus were screaming.

The reinterpretation is that *he was sleeping at the wheel of a bus* which is the basis for the 2nd story, *that the grandfather died in a bus wreck after falling asleep at the wheel causing the kids to scream.* This, in turn, is communicated as the punch "But the kids on his bus were screaming."

Diagram 4 shows you where the reinterpretation fits on the Joke Diagram.

Diagram 4

My grandfather died peacefully in his sleep.

Setup

> **1st story:** *The grandfather was at home sleeping when he died of natural causes.*
>
> **Target Assumption:** *He was sleeping in his bed.*
>
> **Reinterpretation:** *He was sleeping at the wheel of a bus.*
>
> **2nd story:** *The grandfather died in a bus wreck after falling asleep at the wheel causing the kids to scream.*
>
> But the kids on his bus were screaming.

Punch

2. The reinterpretation reveals an unexpected interpretation of the thing about which the target assumption is made. Within the setup, there's some *thing* about which the audience makes the target assumption. If you investigate Diagram 4 you'll discover that *the sleeping grandfather* is the *thing* that caused you to make the target assumption *he was sleeping in his bed*, as well as the reinterpretation that *he was sleeping at the wheel of the bus*.

These two interpretations of one *thing* are essential to making a joke work. When a punch presents a reinterpretation, the audience is confronted with an unexpected yet compatible interpretation of the thing within the setup. This makes them review their assumptions until they identify the one that is wrong, thus shattering that target assumption.

SECRET #3:

THE AIM OF THE REINTERPRETATION IS TO SHATTER THE TARGET ASSUMPTION.

Shattering the target assumption with an unexpected reinterpretation is what creates surprise. When your joke shatters people's assumptions, they laugh. Now we're back where we began: expectation and surprise. Only now you understand how the mechanisms of target assumption and reinterpretation cause them to happen.

REINTERPRETATION: JOKES WITHOUT PUNCHES

Now you may be thinking, "So if the punch must contain a reinterpretation, what about jokes that don't have punch lines?" It may seem odd, but there are some jokes that don't require an expressed punch. An example of this is the following joke where the setup leads to an inevitable, obvious punch:

> I went to this expensive restaurant that had a waiter for everything. The *water* waiter gave me *water*. The *coffee* waiter gave me *coffee*. The *head* waiter. . .

How did you complete this joke? Naughty, naughty. The reinterpretation, about the speaker receiving oral sex, is so strongly implied it doesn't need to be spelled out in the punch. The audience members supply the reinterpretation, which shatters the target assumption. However, because a joke allows the audience to infer the punch doesn't mean the fundamentals of target assumption and reinterpretation don't apply: They do.

WHERE DO REINTERPRETATIONS COME FROM?

First, you must understand that everything has many possible interpretations. Any interpretation other than the assumed one is a reinterpretation. For instance, words can have multiple interpretations, as with this joke:

> I went to my doctor for shingles—he sold me aluminum siding.

Notice how the word *shingles* has multiple meanings. The assumed interpretation—that *shingles means skin condition*—is the target; the unexpected interpretation—that *shingles means house covering*—is the reinterpretation.

In addition, objects can be interpreted in many ways. For instance, I've seen several comics do the sight gag of pretending to be on a beach, then use the mike stand as if it's a metal detector. The target assumption is that *the metal pole with the round thing on the end is for holding a microphone*; and the reinterpretation is that *the metal pole with the round thing on the end is a metal detector*.

Reinterpretations come from the kind of mind that notices what others assume, then uncovers or invents alternative interpretations. To do this, funny people must be able to interpret one *thing* in two ways.

Connector:
One Thing Interpreted in At Least Two Ways

At the center of joke structure is a third mechanism which I call the *connector*, defined as *one thing interpreted in at least two ways*. Interpreting the connector in one way provides the target assumption, and interpreting it in another supplies the reinterpretation.

In the "grandfather" joke, the connector is *the sleeping grandfather*. It's the one *thing* interpreted in two ways, as you can see when you view Diagram 5.

Diagram 5

My grandfather died peacefully in his sleep.

Setup	
	1st Story: *The grandfather was at home sleepng when he died of natural causes.* **Target Assumption:** *He was sleeping in his bed.* **Connector:** *The sleeping grandfather.* **Reinterpretation:** *He was sleeping at the wheel of a bus.* **2nd story:** *The grandfather died in a bus wreck after falling asleep at the wheel causing the kids to scream.* But the kids on his bus were screaming.

Punch

Notice the definition of the connector includes "in *at least* two ways." Connectors can have many possible interpretations; two is simply the minimum required to construct a joke. When a connector can be interpreted in several ways, it can result in a joke with multiple punches. This brings us to the connector's requirement: The connector must be only *one thing.*

Jokes are rather simple structures because they revolve around one central idea. If there's more than one connector, there's more than one joke. Think about it: Two connectors would lead to two target assumptions and two reinterpretations, which in turn would require two setups and two punches, hence two jokes. One connector per joke is all you need.

Since any *thing* can be a connector, the challenge is in recognizing it. As we discussed in the previous section on reinterpretation, words and objects lend themselves to multiple interpretations, so they make excellent connectors. For the joke "I went to my doctor for shingles—he sold me aluminum siding," the connector is the word *shingles*, because it's the one thing interpreted as both a *skin condition* and *house covering*. As for the microphone stand sight gag, the connector is the *mike stand* because it can be used for *holding a microphone* or as a *metal detector*.

Not all jokes are constructed with just words and objects; here is an example from a silent movie comedy, using only body language as a connector. Picture this scene: A wealthy drunkard in his parlor finds a note from his wife saying she's left him and won't return until he stops drinking. He turns away from the camera, and walks to a counter. He hangs his head, and his shoulders begin shaking up and down spasmodically. He's sobbing, right? Crying his eyes out over losing her? Nope. He turns around, and we see he's shaking up a drink in a martini mixer. Can you figure out the connector before you look at Diagram 6?

Diagram 6

A wealthy drunkard in his parlor finds a note from his wife saying she left him, and won't come back unless he stops drinking. He turns away from the camera and walks over to a counter. He hangs his head, and his shoulders begin shaking up and down spasmodically.

Setup

    1st Story: *He's upset because his wife left him because he's an alcoholic.*

    Target Assumption: *He's crying.*

    Connector: *The shaking of his shoulders.*

    Reinterpretation: *He's mixing a drink.*

    2nd Story: *He's more interested in drinking than his wife.*

    He turns around, and we see he's shaking up a drink in a martini mixer.

Punch

This is perfect joke structure using only body language, with the connector being *the shaking of his shoulders.* That motion is the thing that causes you to make the target assumption that *he's crying.* Then *the shaking of his shoulders* is reinterpreted and reveals that actually *he's mixing a drink.* By the way, that scene is from a Charlie Chaplin film called *The Idle Class.*

Now I know you're saying to yourself, "That's great, but it isn't true for *all* jokes." I beg to disagree. These fundamentals of joke structure are the same for all jokes. It doesn't matter whether the laugh emanates from the wit of a literary story, a clown's pratfall, a remark in a situation comedy, a dirty joke, an accidental humorous irony, an off-handed comment at a party, a funny riddle, or a gag without an overt setup or punch—the underlying structure is the same.

The problem in recognizing these fundamentals is that there are so many joke format variations. The structure is often masked by the nature of the character performing the joke, hidden deep within cultural or national presuppositions, obscured by layers of implication, and disguised by individual styles of expression. But no matter the variation, the 1st story and target assumption, the connector, and the 2nd story and reinterpretation are essential in constructing *all* jokes. In time, you'll become proficient at identifying them and a whole new universe of joke possibilities will open up.

It's imperative that you thoroughly comprehend the mechanisms of joke structure before moving onto Chapter 2. If you don't, reread this chapter until you do, because these are the tools you'll need to dig into my joke writing system, *the Joke Prospector.* Understanding these fundamentals will help you find the humor in things because you now know how a joke works. (But don't worry, I won't make you diagram your jokes as you did sentences in grade school!)

2

Joke Writing
The Joke Prospector

Can anyone learn to write jokes? Yes!

For some reason, there seems to be a forbidding aura around joke writing, as if it's some mystical act that only those blessed by Thelia, the Muse of Comedy, can accomplish. Everyone is funny sometimes, even if only by accident. Just because you don't know *how* you're creating a joke doesn't mean you're not creating one. In this chapter, I'm going to show you how to make those wonderful accidents happen whenever you want.

Still have doubts? Fine. (If you don't have *any* doubts you're probably a little too trusting. Stay away from those late night infomercials.) Consider this: In the previous chapter you learned that all jokes have an easily recognizable and knowable structure. If joke structure is knowable, it stands to reason that joke writing is doable.

Every joke writing system lends itself to writing one-liners. (Why they're called one-liners when they have two lines, I'll never understand.) Interestingly, the vast majority of jokes in the world come from social situations as jokes *without* setups. But jokes *without* setups are nearly impossible to teach without first understanding the makeup and composition of jokes *with* setups. Therefore, the Joke Prospector writing system deals exclusively with jokes *with* setups. Once you comprehend these, it will be much easier for you to write jokes *without* setups, which will eventually evolve into comedic story telling.

The *Joke Prospector* is an original joke writing system that takes you step by step from a joke topic to a completed joke. I named it the Joke Prospector because it consists of two distinct phases: the *Joke Map* and the *Joke Mine*.

The Joke Map is designed to help you decide on a topic, define a punch–premise, a setup–premise, and from that idea write some joke

15

setups. Then the Joke Mine digs into a setup and uses the target assumption, connector, and reinterpretation to create a punch.

Because this is a step-by-step system that models how jokes are formed in the mind, it requires a bit of explanation. Rest assured, however, that once you get the basic gist of how the Joke Prospector works, the jokes will flow.

You'll be working with the two phases of the Joke Prospector in reverse order. From teaching the system, I've found that the process of joke construction is much clearer when you begin by writing punches for setups, so we'll start in this chapter with the Joke Mine. Once you learn how the Joke Mine works, you can practice writing some punches of your own for setups I've provided on the exercise sheets at the end of this chapter. When you've gained some experience doing that, it will be much easier to learn how to use the Joke Map (see Chapter 3) to help choose a subject for your material and write some setups. This, in turn, will lead you right back to the Joke Mine to write punches for those setups. (More exercise sheets covering the entire Joke Prospector system are at the end of Chapter 3.)

The Joke Mine:
Exploring the Secret Passageway

Digging into the Joke Mine, you'll learn to write jokes by going through a secret passageway that leads from setup to punch. Most people don't know about this passageway, and even when you get to know it, its many twists and turns will still take you to unexpected places. That's the fun of a journey through the Joke Mine. Like Alice in Wonderland when she went down the rabbit hole, you'll find a world that gets "curiouser and curiouser."

How do you explore this secret passageway?

SECRET #4:
YOU EXPLORE A JOKE'S PASSAGEWAYS BY ASKING QUESTIONS.

Asking questions is the best way to stay focused on your search for a good tunnel. Beginning joke writers often get stuck saying the same things in their heads over and over again, such as, "What's funny about this? What's funny about this?" or "Where's the joke? Where's the joke?" That gets you nowhere.

If you're ever going to find a tunnel that leads to pay dirt, you have to hunt around the mine a little, not just stand in one place scratching your nuggets. Your mind needs a constant supply of new information to sift through in search of humor. This flow of information stops when you're stuck in a self-talk loop. Asking questions forces you to come up with answers, and each answer will take you farther along your way or even lead to a completely different tunnel. You can't know ahead of time which tunnel will lead to a punch you'll like, so the trick is to ask *lots* of questions. If a particular answer doesn't lead to a joke, at least you'll know that you examined that tunnel and decided not to go in that direction. Any exploration is better than being stuck saying the same thing over and over again. Any exploration is better than being stuck saying the same thing over and over again. Any exploration is better than being stuck . . . you get the point.

I'm bringing this up now because in order to get the raw material you'll need to complete the steps in the following list, you'll have to ask questions. One or more questions accompany each of the five steps; others you'll have to make up for yourself. Most comedians are not even aware that they're asking themselves questions. But on some level, consciously or unconsciously, they are. How else could they continually come up with new information and ideas to develop jokes? So I want you to begin asking questions consciously. When you learn to do that, you may excavate some deeply buried riches that will surprise you as well as your audience. The steps making up the Joke Mine are:

1. Select a setup, then list the assumptions: "What am I assuming about this statement?"
2. Pick a target assumption, and identify the connector: "What is the thing that caused me to make this target assumption?"
3. List some reinterpretations for the connector: "Other than the target, what other interpretations are there for my connector?"
4. Choose a reinterpretation, and compose a 2nd story: "Relative to the setup, what specific situation could explain my reinterpretation?"

5. Write a punch that expresses the 2nd story: "In addition to the setup, what information is needed to communicate my 2nd story clearly?"

From Setup to Punch

As you move through the Joke Mine, I'd like to state one thing loud and clear. (Maybe you can't hear how loud I am, but I do want you to be clear about this point.) *If at any time in this process you think of a joke, write it down.* The purpose of this system is to help you generate material. A good joke is a good joke, no matter how or when you compose it. It doesn't matter if it's the result of going through all the Joke Mine steps, or just doing the first step, or even having a random thought. If you think it's a good idea or joke, write it down.

The first step in the Joke Mine is the setup. Let's start with this one:

1. SELECT A SETUP, THEN LIST THE ASSUMPTIONS: "WHAT AM I ASSUMING ABOUT THIS STATEMENT?"

> This morning I got up and ran five miles.

You've made assumptions about the setup, though you may not be aware of them. To find out what they are, examine the details of the 1st story that you imagined. Any difference between what the setup actually says and the 1st story is an assumption. Now ask this step's question:

Q: What am I assuming about this statement?
A: I'm assuming:
    a. He ran in order to get exercise.
    b. He's not exaggerating about the distance.
    c. He's running outside.
    d. *I ran* means he jogged on his own feet.
    e. He's telling the truth.

These assumptions aren't the only ones that could be made, and they're not necessarily the "right ones." They're just the ones that are obvious to me. (Whenever you work with any of the step's questions, be sure to write your answers down. Don't try to keep them all in your head. Many people automatically come up with jokes by just gleaning assumptions. If you do, write them down, too.)

The next step in the Joke Mine is:

18

2. Pick a Target Assumption, and Identify the Connector: "What is the thing that caused me to make this target assumption?" My impulse is to go with (a) because it's the most obvious:

Target Assumption: *He ran in order to get exercise.*

When pondering which assumption to pick as your target assumption, consider the one that lends itself to the most humor. If you find yourself instinctively drawn to a particular target, trust your impulse; if you notice a target that indicates a reinterpretation with comical possibilities, go for it.

Often the most obvious assumption is usually the best choice for the target assumption because it's the one everybody will make when you deliver the setup. Remember, you want to eventually shatter the assumption held by your audience. That won't be possible if you choose an obscure assumption that most of the audience members won't make.

Once you've picked your target assumption, you need to identify the thing that you made the assumption about: the connector. This is the most important and difficult step in this system. After you've identified the connector, all of the following steps are an extension of it. Take the time to evaluate your thought process up to this point. Some essential ingredient in the setup caused you to make your target assumption. What was it? The best tool you have for identifying it is the question for this step:

Q: What is the thing that caused me to make this target assumption?
A: If my target assumption is *he ran in order to get exercise*, then I made this assumption about the *reason* he ran.

Connector: *The reason he ran.*

So now *the reason he ran* is the connector, the thing you're making the target assumption about. In the next step, we will look at other interpretations of this connector, which will help to understand how *the reason he ran* can be interpreted in at least two different ways.

As we go along, I'll continue putting our information on the Joke Diagram. (You don't have to do this when you're writing your own jokes.) This shows how each step supplies a different part of the joke. (See Diagram 7.)

Diagram 7

This morning I got up and ran five miles.

Setup

> **1st Story:** *He's a healthy go-getter.*
> **Target Assumption:** *He ran in order to get exercise.*
>
> **Connector:** *The reason he ran.*
>
> **Reinterpretation:** *?*
> **2nd Story:** *?*

Punch

3. List Some Reinterpretations for the Connector: "Other than the target, what other interpretations are there for my connector?"

What we're looking for are alternative interpretations for the connector *the reason he ran*. The key here is to be as specific as possible. For instance, instead of just saying *"He was scared,"* try imagining a more detailed situation, such as *He ran because he was scared by a horrifying face*. Ask the step's question:

Q: Other than the target, what other interpretations are there for my connector (*the reason he ran*)?
A: Other possible reasons for the subject running five miles could be:
  a. He ran because he was scared by a horrifying face.
  b. He ran because he was being pulled along against his will.
  c. He ran because he was chasing a naked woman.
  d. He ran because his car was rolling away.

Keep in mind that these are neither the only reinterpretations nor the "right ones." The list could have been longer, I'm sure, and no doubt you will come up with interpretations I didn't think of. Also, if some of these sound goofy, bizarre, or implausible relative to the setup, it's all right. When you're prospecting, not everything will yield ore. This leads us to the next step.

4. CHOOSE A REINTERPRETATION, AND COMPOSE A 2ND STORY: "RELATIVE TO THE SETUP, WHAT SPECIFIC SITUATION COULD EXPLAIN MY REINTERPRETATION?"

In this step, you select one of the reinterpretations from the list, and it becomes your joke's reinterpretation. I'm choosing (a).

Reinterpretation: *He ran because he was scared by a horrifying face.*

This reinterpretation by itself isn't usually a punch, but it is the central concept for the 2nd story. Note that the reinterpretation derives its meaning relative to the setup: *This morning he got up and ran five miles (because he was scared by a horrifying face).* This is important to check because not all reinterpretations are plausible ideas for a punch.

To devise a 2nd story, you'll need to search through various situations that will help explain or justify the reinterpretation. The question from this step may be sufficient to enable you to do this, you might have to ask a number of questions, or the idea might come without asking any questions at all. If suddenly you think of a punch that works, write it down. However, it's best to be prepared to keep digging with questions until you find the situation and story you need. Let's start with the step's question:

Q: Relative to the setup, what specific situation could explain my reinterpretation?
A: He woke up in bed with an ugly person.

That's a situation, but for the punch to make complete sense, it will need more details. Let's keep digging:

Q: Why did he wake up in bed with an ugly person?
A: He might have spent the night with an ugly lady.
Q: Why would he do that?
A: He picked her up in a bar the night before when he was really drunk.

That was easy. Now let's put it all together as a 2nd story:

The night before, he got really drunk in a bar, picked up an ugly lady, and spent the night with her. In the morning, when he woke up sober and had a chance to see what she actually looked like, he bolted.

If you come up with a different story, that's fine as long as it explains in a believable way how a horrifying face that scared him happened to be there when he woke up. Diagram 8 shows the information we have so far.

Diagram 8
This morning I got up and ran five miles.

Setup	**1st Story:** *He's a healthy go-getter.* **Target Assumption:** *He ran in order to get exercise.* **Connector:** *The reason he ran.* **Reinterpretation:** *He ran because he was scared by a horrifying face.* **2nd Story:** *He woke up next to an ugly bar pickup and bolted.*

Punch

We've made it all the way through the passage. We started with the setup, which gave us our 1st story. Then we went on to dig up a target assumption, a connector, and a reinterpretation, and composed a plausible 2nd story. Now we're ready to excavate a punch.

5. WRITE A PUNCH THAT EXPRESSES THE 2ND STORY: "IN ADDITION TO THE SETUP, WHAT INFORMATION IS NEEDED TO COMMUNICATE MY 2ND STORY CLEARLY?"
There are many ways to communicate the 2nd story as a punch. In addition to deciding what the punch should say, you'll need to experiment with how it should be phrased or acted out. Asking questions is the best way to come up with ideas, so begin with the step's question, then keep digging with more questions until you unearth a gem.

Q: In addition to the setup, what information is needed to communicate my 2nd story clearly?
A: He picked up someone ugly in a bar, woke up next to her, and that's why he ran.

This is the information that the punch has to get across. It must do so effectively but, at the same time, concisely. That's why writing a good punch is sort of like solving a puzzle. The solution is to say only what's needed to communicate the 2nd story clearly. Here are a few guidelines for writing a punch:

- There is no one "right way" to go about writing a punch. How a punch is phrased or acted out will change from comedian to comedian. Write punches in the way you naturally speak or act.
- Since brevity is the soul of wit, you should try to reveal the 2nd story in as *few words as possible*.

Take this punch, for example:

This morning I got up and ran five miles. That's because I was in a bar last night, and I picked up this incredibly ugly woman when I was dead drunk. I spent the night with her, but when I saw her this morning I freaked.

Although this punch does reveal and communicate our 2nd story, it doesn't do so succinctly. That's why it doesn't sound very funny. As the name suggests, a punch really should be like a blow from a fist—hard and fast. I like this one better:

This morning I got up and ran five miles. You would've too, if you rolled over and saw the troll I picked up last night at that bar.

This version is not only a full eighteen words shorter, but it saves the most surprising aspect for *the end* of the punch. This increases the impact tremendously.

So how do you decide on the exact wording for a punch? Let your sense of humor be your guide. Try many different versions, then go with the phrasing that sounds funniest to *you*.

Diagram 9 shows the final version of our joke. Look through all the steps and observe the comic logic that takes us through the passage from setup to punch.

Diagram 9

This morning I got up and ran five miles.

Setup	
	1st Story: *He's a healthy go-getter.*
	Target Assumption: *He ran in order to get exercise.*
	Connector: *The reason he ran.*
	Reinterpretation: *He ran because he was scared by a horrifying face.*
	2nd Story: *He woke up next to an ugly bar pickup and bolted.*
	You would have too, if you rolled over and saw the troll I picked up last night at that bar.

Punch

Remember, you only have to give the audience enough information to get the 2nd story across. How you do it is entirely up to you. It doesn't even have to be done with words—for instance, the joke we just wrote could also be written this way:

> This morning I got up and ran five miles. It was like . . . *(pantomime waking up with a terrible hangover, turning over, seeing an ugly bar pickup, tearing your arm free, and running).*

If you have the acting skills to make the audience envision the scene from your physical reenactment alone, that's all they'll need to put the 2nd story together. That's what I mean by there being no single "right way."

I can tell you quite honestly that when I started writing this joke I had absolutely no idea where it would end up, but the punch isn't bad at all. That's the rabbit hole for you. And speaking of rabbit holes, I want to show you how you can come up with different punches by exploring different tunnels.

Joke Mine Options: Exploring Other Tunnels

What happens when, no matter how you try to phrase it or act it out, you don't like the joke you come out of the passage with? Or what if you get stuck in a tunnel and can't find a way out, no matter how hard you try? What do you do then? Well, there are always jobs available in the food service industry. And, you have a few other options.

When you get stuck or come up with a joke you don't much care for, don't panic. Just return to Step 4 and choose another reinterpretation until you find one that makes you laugh. If you're still not happy, go all the way back to Step 2 and pick another target assumption. Each alternative represents another tunnel that could lead to a joke you'll like.

GO BACK TO STEP 4: CHOOSE A DIFFERENT REINTERPRETATION
For this variation, I'm going to streamline my explanation. This method can provide plenty of unexplored tunnels to search whenever you feel the need for change of direction.

This is the setup statement:

This morning I got up and ran five miles.

And here's the information from the first three steps:

Target assumption: *He ran in order to get exercise.*
Connector: *The reason he ran.*
Reinterpretations: a. *He ran because he was scared by a horrifying face.*
                    b. *He ran because he was being pulled along against his will.*
                    c. *He ran because he was chasing a naked woman.*
                    d. *His ran because his car was rolling away.*

4. CHOOSE A REINTERPRETATION, AND COMPOSE A 2ND STORY: "RELATIVE TO THE SETUP, WHAT SPECIFIC SITUATION COULD EXPLAIN MY REINTERPRETATION?"
This time let's choose (b) from the list of possibilities.

Reinterpretation: *He ran because he was being pulled along against his will.*

Now ask the step's question:

Q: Relative to the setup, what specific situation could explain my reinterpretation?

A: He could be pulled along by a train.

After asking a number of questions in an attempt to build a 2nd story that would make sense of this reinterpretation, I came up with this:

> While riding on a train, he fell out of the sleeper car, got hooked on the door, and had to run alongside the train.

5. Write a Punch That Expresses the 2nd Story: "In addition to the setup, what information is needed to communicate my 2nd story clearly?"
In answer to this step's question, I wrote this punch:

> This morning I got up and ran five miles. While riding on a train, I rolled over in my berth and fell out of the sleeper car, and my pajama top got caught on the door.

In my professional opinion, that sucks. It's not believable at all, and I wouldn't perform this joke or even admit I wrote it to anyone—except you, of course. But it serves to demonstrate that when you're prospecting for the mother lode, sometimes you only come up with fool's gold. After all, I don't want to give you the impression that all the jokes created with this system are great ones. Some will be great, some will be okay, and some will bite the big one. That's the nature of joke writing. The idea is to have options.

Here, for instance, we've ended up with a joke that's pretty awful. But with a different reinterpretation or target assumption, we might come up with something better. So let's go back to Step 4 and choose another reinterpretation.

Go Back to Step 4 Again: Choose Another Reinterpretation
I'm going to go through this with even less explanation because if you're not clear about how this system works by now, you should consider a job that requires a shovel.

4. Choose a Reinterpretation, and Compose a 2nd Story: "Relative to the setup, what specific situation could explain my reinterpretation?"
Going down the list, we'll pick reinterpretation (d):

> Reinterpretation: *He ran because his car was rolling away.*

After asking the step's question and several more about how the speaker could wind up chasing his own car, I came up with this 2nd story:

His battery died, and when he push-started the car all by himself, it took off downhill and he had to chase it.

This struck me as a good story, but it seemed to conflict slightly with the setup's implication that the speaker had just awakened. That would seem to place him in a bedroom rather than outside with his car. This wasn't really a problem, though, and in a second you'll see why.

5. WRITE A PUNCH THAT EXPRESSES THE 2ND STORY: "IN ADDITION TO THE SETUP, WHAT INFORMATION IS NEEDED TO COMMUNICATE MY 2ND STORY CLEARLY?"

When I answered this question to help me create a punch that would effectively express my 2nd story, I also adjusted the setup to fit the 2nd story better. This was the result:

This morning I got up, went out, and ran five miles. Never push-start your car when you're alone on a hill.

Diagram 10 shows what this one looks like.

Diagram 10

This morning I got up, went out, and ran five miles.

Setup

1st Story: *He's a healthy go-getter.*
Target Assumption: *He ran in order to get exercise.*

Connector: *The reason he ran.*

Reinterpretation: *He ran because his car was rolling away.*
2nd Story: *His battery died, and when he push-started the car all by himself, it took off downhill and he had to chase it.*

Never push start your car when you're alone on a hill.

Punch

This joke tickles me, and I'd say it's a keeper. Eureka!

Occasionally, you'll come up with a great 2nd story that seems to clash with some little detail in the setup. If that happens, make whatever adjustments are needed for the joke to work. When it comes to joke writing, nothing is set in stone. It's your joke, and you can change it any way that suits you. In this case, simply adding the words *went out* to the setup placed the speaker outside and suggested that he hadn't just rolled out of bed. At the same time, it didn't alter the 1st story, target assumption, or connector.

I can't begin to cover all the ways a joke can be written and rewritten, so I'll do the next best thing: encourage you to experiment.

Between this punch and the one about the bar pickup, we've written two good jokes by digging different tunnels through the passage. But let's say that you still don't like any of the punches we've come up with (and maybe you don't). What do you do then? There's still the option of going all the way back to Step 2 and choosing a different target assumption.

Go Back to Step 2: Pick a Different Target Assumption
Our original setup was:

> This morning I got up and ran five miles.

Here's the list of assumptions we compiled in Step 1:
a. He ran in order to get exercise.
b. He's not exaggerating about the distance.
c. He's running outside.
d. *I ran* means he jogged on his own feet.
e. He's telling the truth.

You should be familiar with how the steps work by now. What I really want you to notice is how choosing a different target assumption will lead you to a different punch.

2. Pick a Target Assumption, and Identify the Connector: "What is the thing that caused me to make this target assumption?"
This time I'm going to try target assumption (e).

> Target Assumption: *He's telling the truth.*

Q: What is the thing that caused me to make this target assumption?
A: His manner of communicating.

Connector: *His manner of communicating.*

I know that *his manner of communicating* is the connector because it's what caused me to make the target assumption *he's telling the truth.* Another indication that *his manner of communicating* is the connector is the fact that it can be interpreted in more than one way.

3. LIST SOME REINTERPRETATIONS FOR THE CONNECTOR: "OTHER THAN THE TARGET, WHAT OTHER INTERPRETATIONS ARE THERE FOR MY CONNECTOR?"
Ask this step's question:

Q: Other than the target, what other interpretations are there for my connector (his manner of communication)?
A: *a. He's lying and didn't actually run that far or at all.*

Sometimes the possibilities are singular.

4. CHOOSE A REINTERPRETATION, AND COMPOSE A 2ND STORY: "REL-ATIVE TO THE SETUP, WHAT SPECIFIC SITUATION COULD EXPLAIN MY RE-INTERPRETATION?"
Ummm . . . I'll choose (a).

Reinterpretation: *He's lying and didn't actually run that far or at all.*

Asking this step's question and a few more give me the details I need to create a believable 2nd story that explains how this guy could justify saying he ran five miles when he didn't actually run at all:

He's bragging about being so wealthy that he can hire someone else to do his jogging for him.

5. WRITE A PUNCH THAT EXPRESSES THE 2ND STORY: "IN ADDITION TO THE SETUP, WHAT INFORMATION IS NEEDED TO COMMUNICATE MY 2ND STORY CLEARLY?"
In answer to this step's question I wrote this joke:

"This morning I got up and ran five miles. Well, not me personal-ly; I pay a guy to do that for me.

Diagram 11 illustrates the whole joke.

Diagram 11

This morning I got up and ran five miles.

Setup	**1st Story:** *He's a healthy go-getter.* **Target Assumption:** *He's telling the truth.* **Connector:** *That he actually ran the five miles.* **Reinterpretation:** *He's lying and didn't actually run that far or at all.* **2nd Story:** *He's a wealthy guy who hires someone to jog for him.* Well, not me personally, I pay a guy to do that for me.

Punch

That's not too bad, especially for a heavy-set comic. Louie Anderson could probably get a nice laugh from a joke like that. This example shows how going back to Step 2 and choosing a different target assumption can lead to a different joke.

What if, after going all the way through the passage and exploring different tunnels by choosing alternate reinterpretations or target assumptions, you still haven't hit pay dirt or hate the punches you've come up with? In the next chapter I'll cover selecting another setup in the Joke Map section.

So far we've managed to develop a couple of decent punches from one setup—a pretty good strike. That's the beauty of using this joke system; you don't have to sit around waiting for a lightning bolt of inspiration. Of course you'll still think of jokes out of the blue sometimes, but if you write every day or need something funny right away, you'll know how to go through the passageway and find it.

The Joke Mine has as many tunnels as your imagination will allow you to explore. It's designed to be flexible and help you express your sense of humor. All you have to do is spend some time digging for it.

Now that you've learned about the elements of joke structure, it's time for you to enter the Joke Mine to explore the secret passage between setup and punch. Using a separate piece of paper, plug the following setups into the form on page 32 and write a punch for each setup.

Setups: I drove through an exclusive neighborhood.
I was stuck in a hospital for a week.
For Father's Day, I took my father out.

Practicing the Joke Mine

1. Select a Setup, Then List the Assumptions: "What am I assuming about this statement?"

   Setup: _____

   Assumptions: _____

2. Pick a Target Assumption, and Identify the Connector: "What is the thing that caused me to make this target assumption?"

   Target: _____

   Connector: _____

3. List Some Reinterpretations for the Connector: "Other than the target, what other interpretations are there for my connector?"

   Reinterpretations: _____

4. Choose a Reinterpretation, and Compose a 2nd Story: "Relative to the setup, what specific situation could explain my reinterpretation?"

   Setup: _____

   Reinterpretation: _____

   2nd Story: _____

5. Write a Punch That Expresses the 2nd Story: "In addition to the setup, what information is needed to communicate my 2nd story clearly?"

   Setup: _____

   Punch: _____

3

What to Write Jokes About
The Joke Prospector

Every working comic has been asked the question, "Where do you get the ideas for your material?" The answer, of course, is "from *my* life." I say that because I don't know anything about *your* life.

There's an old writing adage that says, "Write what you know." And, really, if you think about it, what else can you write? As an artist you have one incredibly precious thing that no one else in the entire world has: your own perspective. That's why I urge you to write about *your* world as *you* perceive it, the things that interest you, and your own opinions and feelings. Tell *your* truth. Whether the audience agrees with you is not an issue. Many artists, from Picasso to Andrew "Dice" Clay, have expressed points of view that ran counter to their peers'. They told *their* truth, and people—eventually a lot of people—responded to that truth. (Even though Picasso never did appear on Letterman.)

One thing you should never, ever try to write about is *what you guess the audience might think is funny.* There's actually a word for people who only try to write what they think someone else will like: *Hacks.*

You do have to consider whether the audience will be able to understand what you say. But always rely on your own sensibilities to guide you when you're making the initial decisions about what's funny, interesting, important, or simply worth talking about. If you really think there's something terribly funny about McNuggets, PMS, farting, pee-pee, snot, or butt-thongs, then by all means write about those things. But don't do it because you heard someone else get a laugh with it.

Many comedians never actively choose what they're going to write jokes about because they wait for inspiration. A new routine comes to them all at once in an unpredictable flash of funny thoughts. Then they dry up until the next lightning bolt strikes. These comics rely only on this haphazard approach because they don't know any other way.

In my opinion, inspiration is without a doubt the best way to generate material. The subject matter is heartfelt and honest, and the jokes are usually well-structured because they come in an intuitive flash. However, if you want to be able to write material on a topic of your choice at any time, you need a method. And, as you know, I just happen to have one: The Joke Prospector.

The Joke Map

In the previous chapter, we dug into the Joke Mine to find punches for setups. Here, I'll explain how the *Joke Map* allows you to survey your life for the raw material that will lead to joke setups. Then we'll reenter the Joke Mine to find punches for them. If you're starting from nothing, the realization that you can write jokes about *everything* can be overwhelming. The Joke Map assists you in turning generalities into specifics, which is essential because . . .

SECRET 5:

THE JOKES ARE IN THE DETAILS.

I cannot overemphasize the importance of this secret. When my students have difficulty writing material, it's usually because they're attempting to find a joke in some broad generality. As soon as they begin searching in the details, they discover treasure. As the father of acting technique, Constantine Stanislavski, once said, "Generality is the death of art." This also applies to writing comedy—you can never be too specific.

Narrowing your ideas from generalities to specific details is the primary function of the Joke Map. This is accomplished in five steps, helping you move from a chosen *topic* to creating a *punch–premise* to forming a *setup–premise*, and then writing some setups.

Topic: Single Subject Presenting Something "Wrong"

Choosing a joke topic can be either an extremely simple step or an angst-ridden quandary. Simple, because topics are often thrust upon us.

If you are trapped in car hell, ending a relationship, or have been in an earthquake, hurricane, or flood, it's easy to find a topic. However, for those people who are reluctant to express true opinions, finding a topic can present a crisis since it requires them to be vulnerable and specific.

In my advanced workshops, students often search for a topic in areas they think of as fun, and they seldom come up with anything. When they delve into areas where they have conflicts, issues, and problems, they find a wealth of material. Sometimes I ask questions to help them investigate a problem area, and they'll almost always say, "But that's not funny." And they're right. A *topic isn't funny*. It's the hurtful things that lead to funny jokes. Why is it that these unfunny things are such fertile areas for comedy?

SECRET #6:

THE SENSE OF HUMOR EVOLVED AS A MEANS OF COPING WITH PAINFUL THINGS.

Potential comedy hides in the most unlikely places—painful things. Does this mean I'm asking you to write jokes about painful things? Well . . . yes and no. I'm asking you to write jokes about something you consider "wrong."

There's an element of pain in every joke, because things we consider wrong cause us pain in some form, ranging from agony to mild discomfort. Sometimes the pain is as obvious as Richard Pryor's reenactment of his heart attack, and sometimes as subtle as Steven Wright's existential angst. But it's always there. Always.

Let's begin with the joke below and follow how it was written using the Joke Prospector.

The postal workers are actually very efficient—with guns.

When choosing a topic, we must consider if it fits the criteria of being a *single subject presenting something wrong*. Take, for instance, this topic:

Topic: *the post office*

Is it a single subject? Yes. Like a sentence, paragraph, chapter, or story, a joke should have one idea at its core. Any creative endeavor that tries to cover more than one central idea tends to get lost because it has no single through line. Is there something wrong for someone? Yes. Although the issue isn't stated in the topic, it's still the basis for choosing the topic in the first place.

An important note: A *topic must* not *include an opinion*. The function of a topic is to begin with something general, from which you can generate countless details. For instance, if I were to phrase the topic as the post office *is slow*, I am restricted to writing jokes about the post office being slow. As a foundation, it's better to use a broad topic that you can have many opinions about. And don't worry, you'll get a chance to express all your opinions in the punch–premise.

Keep in mind that a topic doesn't have to be something wrong only for you; it can be something wrong for someone or something else. What do I mean by "something else"? For instance, Robin Williams has a bit about changing his baby's diaper, in which the baby poops on the floor. Robin becomes his dog, checks out the situation, and then asks why his owner doesn't rub the *youngster's* nose in it. The dog has a problem with the fact that the child is getting better treatment than he would in a similar circumstance.

Association List: Smaller Aspects

Once you've chosen a general topic, make an association list of all the specific things you can think of relating to that topic. Keep the entries on the list as short as possible and avoid long descriptions. It's important to keep your choices specific; I could list *door*, for example, but that could be an aspect of almost anything. Choose things identified with your topic.

lines	boxes	uniforms	federal building
eagle logo	keys jingle	envelopes	stamp designers
stamps	string	postcards	delivering mail
mail slots	P.O. box	P.O. box key	stamp machines
letters	pony express	packages	wanted posters
mailbox	Express Mail	tellers	postal workers
jeeps	biting dogs	licking	
job security	junk mail	government agency	
employee of the month			
vehicle steering wheel on opposite side			
postal slogan (Neither rain, nor sleet . . .)			

Punch–Premise: A Negative Opinion
About a Smaller Aspect

Assuming you've selected a proper topic, you now need to narrow this idea to a more specific concept which I call a *punch–premise*. The reason I call it the punch–premise is that your punches will, more often than not, be an expression of this concept. The punch-premise is *a negative opinion about a smaller aspect* of the topic. By negative opinion, I mean a bunch of things: negative thoughts, judgments, attitudes, feelings, emotional reactions, beliefs, and values. Since we're starting with something wrong (the topic), we're sure to have some negative opinions. By smaller aspect, I mean all the details directly or indirectly related to the topic. This is where your association list comes into play, because it consists entirely of smaller aspects.

To create a punch–premise, I'll select from the association list the smaller aspect *delivering mail* and add a the negative opinion: *incompetent*.

Punch–premise: *incompetent at delivering mail*

An important note: *The punch–premise* cannot *contain an* example. If it includes an example of *how* the postal workers are incompetent at delivering mail, it restricts the punch–premise to the specific area of that example. Here's a badly formed punch–premise with an example:

Bad Premise: incompetent at delivering mail *by taking it to the wrong house*

This incorrectly constructed punch–premise restricts us to writing jokes only about postal workers being incompetent at finding the correct address, which excludes being incompetent because they are too slow, have erratic schedules, intentionally skip houses, have the wrong neighborhood's mail, or anything else we may wish to write about. A punch–premise consists only of a smaller aspect of the topic and a negative opinion about it.

In the Joke Prospector system, having a well devised punch–premise is the key. If your punch–premise is badly constructed, then the rest of the method will go awry. Take the time to make sure your punch–premise is well formed before moving to the next step.

Setup–Premise:
Opposite Opinion to the Punch–Premise

Since punches are expressions of the punch–premise, to write setups you'll need to form a *setup–premise*, which retains the same smaller aspect of the punch–premise, but shifts to an *opposite opinion*.

Keep this step simple. All you are doing is changing to an opinion opposite from that of the punch–premise. The setup–premise is the concept from which you will write your setups.

Punch–premise: *incompetent at delivering mail*

Setup–premise: *competent at delivering mail*

An important note: *Do not use the setup–premise as the setup itself.* Some people get confused because the setup–premise seems like such a good setup that they write one joke from it, then wonder where to go from there. If the setup–premise is formed correctly, you should be able to write a whole bunch of setups.

Setup And Punch: Opposite (Directly or by Degree)

Charlie Chaplin said a long time ago, "Comedy is two opposite ideas that collide." This is true even today. In general terms, setups and punches are opposite either directly in the form of *good to bad*, or by degree in the form of *bad to worse*. Let's examine this relationship to illuminate the reason for employing a punch–premise and a setup–premise that have opposite opinions.

A joke based on the pattern of good to bad is *directly opposite* because the setup is about something *good*, and the punch is about something *bad*. To see how this works, take a look at this joke from Stephen King. That's right, the famous author of horror novels has a wonderfully wicked sense of humor. The story goes that when asked by a journalist how he came up with such imaginative ideas for his stories, Mr. King answered:

I still have the heart of a little boy . . . in a jar on my desk.

To reveal the opposites, let's break the joke down into its fundamental elements. In general terms, the setup is about the author having the playful, imaginative, and creative spirit of a little boy, which is *good*. Then the punch gives us an opposite view, the author keeping the actual physical heart of a little boy in a pickle jar on his writing desk. I think most people would consider that *bad*.

The other relationship between setup and punch is bad to worse, which is less clear because it's *opposite by degree*. To show you what I mean, here's a joke from my student Derek McKusick:

> Being raised with five sisters can really warp your mind. I was sixteen before I realized I was fat and not just retaining water.

In the setup, Derek is influence so completely by his five sisters that he's deluded into believing he isn't fat when he actually is—which is *bad*. Then, in the punch, at sixteen he awakens to the fact that he really is fat and not just retaining water—which is *worse*.

Whether your jokes go from good to bad or bad to worse, they'll always be moving toward the more negative. If you're uncomfortable with this concept, get used to it because it's a consistently useful technique that will come in handy whenever you're writing jokes.

Writing Setups: Examples of the Setup–Premise

As mentioned earlier, the setup–premise is the idea from which you'll write a series of setups. You can best do this by thinking of examples of the setup–premise and writing them as short sentences. It's important to remember that a setup–premise is *not* a setup. If you write a joke using your setup–premise as a setup, you'll only get one joke. This defeats the purpose of a system designed to generate enough jokes for an entire routine.

Here are several setups based on the sample about the post office:

Setup–premise: competent at delivering mail
   a. The postal workers are actually very efficient
   b. I never get anyone else's mail
   c. They are good about forwarding mail

The above setups are all examples reflecting the post office's competence. This seems simple enough, but there's one deceptive challenge. Since the setup–premise's opinion is the *opposite* from what you actually feel about the subject, you'll probably have to use your imagination to make up fictitious examples. *Competent* is *not* my opinion about mail delivery, but to write the above setups I had to put my personal feelings aside and write some examples *as if* the setup–premise

39

were true. Remember, these are only the setups, and you'll get your chance to state your real opinion in the punches.

Bringing the sample joke back to its original form, notice how I used setup (a) to write the completed joke, "The postal workers are actually very efficient—with guns."

I hope this clarifies the various terms of the Joke Map. If you're unclear about the meaning and use of topic, punch–premise, or setup–premise go back and reread this section. You should be familiar with these elements and their relationship to each other before moving on.

Surveying for Material: From Topic to Setup

In this section we'll go through the entire Joke Prospector system and write an original joke. Beginning with the Joke Map, we'll go from topic to setup, then plug that setup into the Joke Mine and, finally, write a punch.

The steps to the Joke Map are:

A. List Some Topics: "What are some things I consider wrong that I'm interested in talking about?"

B. Select One Topic and Make an Association List: "What are all the things I can think of that relate to my topic?"

C. Create Several Punch–Premises: "What negative opinions do I have about some smaller aspects of my topic?"

D. For Each Punch–Premise Form a Setup–Premise: "What's the opposite opinion to my chosen punch–premise?"

E. Choose a Setup–Premise and Write a List of Setups: "What are some examples or statements that express my setup–premise?"

Remember:

SECRET #4 (AGAIN):
YOU EXPLORE BY ASKING QUESTIONS.

Asking questions is the cornerstone of creativity. The steps contain their own questions to help you get started, but if you feel the need to ask more questions in your search for a topic, punch–premise, setup–premise, or setups, by all means do so.

Before unfolding the Joke Map and consulting your comedy compass, there's one more thing to keep in mind. Anywhere within the Joke Prospector you may find that a joke just pops into your mind. That's wonderful. The whole point of this process is to give you a way to generate material. I don't care if you start writing jokes in the middle of the steps. Just because they didn't come directly from the steps of the Joke Prospector doesn't mean they aren't good jokes. Trust yourself: They're probably great jokes. Accept the gift, and write them all down. This joke writing system is built on the principle that when you feed information to a fertile comic mind, it starts cranking out jokes. Go with it. Now, let's get down to the business of writing a joke.

A. LIST SOME TOPICS: "WHAT ARE SOME THINGS I CONSIDER WRONG THAT I'M INTERESTED IN TALKING ABOUT?"
To add a little outside influence to this Joke Map, I asked my friend and co-comedy clinician, Frank Miles, to supply the examples for this section. As always, begin by asking the step's question:

Q: What are some things I consider wrong that I'm interested in talking about?
A: Topics: a. fear
              b. The Department of Motor Vehicles
              c. my family
              d. hockey

Remember, these are Frank's issues; you may have a completely different list.

B. SELECT ONE TOPIC AND MAKE AN ASSOCIATION LIST: "WHAT ARE ALL THE THINGS I CAN THINK OF THAT RELATE TO MY TOPIC?"
Choose the topic for which you have the most emotional heat. Frank's got a lot of issues with his family, so he chose:

Topic: *my family*

Next, an association list is compiled to generate some specific ideas about the topic *my family*. To do this, ask the step's question:

Q: What are all the things I can think of that relate to my topic?

41

A: List: my mother
         my father
         my brother
         family vacations
         family dinners
         family reunions

Frank's original list went on forever because the topic is so broad, but this shortened version will do. Make your own association list as long as possible, and while you're working on it make sure to have extra paper nearby. You may come up with several funny ideas, jokes, or even an entire routine. What you write on the list can stimulate your comic mind, and the next thing you know an entire funny story comes flowing out. It's all part of the process. Enjoy it.

C. CREATE SEVERAL PUNCH–PREMISES: "WHAT NEGATIVE OPINIONS DO I HAVE ABOUT SOME SMALLER ASPECTS OF MY TOPIC?"
Pay close attention to the criteria for creating a punch–premise. Remember, it must have a negative opinion about a smaller aspect of the topic, and it cannot contain an example. These points are very important because this is the step where many students get off course. If you veer off just a few degrees you'll go farther and farther off course as you travel along. Check your punch–premise several times. If you're wondering where to find a smaller aspect of the topic, check your association list. It's full of them.

Ask the step's question:

Q: What negative opinions do I have about some smaller aspects of my topic (*my family*)?
A: Punch–Premises: a. My relationship with my mother was very bad.
                      b. My father was stupid.
                      c. My brother ruined things.
                      d. Our family vacations were hell.

Double-check the punch–premises. Do these involve a more specific aspect of your topic? Yes. Do they include a negative opinion? Yes. Do they contain an example? No. These are valid punch–premises. While these are all based on items from Frank's association list, keep in mind that this may not always be the case. There are many more smaller aspects from which to write punch–premises.

One recurring mistake my students make is getting so excited by how strong a punch–premise is because of the opinion involved that they use it as a setup. This may work, but since a punch–premise can yield many jokes, set your sights on writing an entire routine.

D. For Each Punch–Premise Form a Setup–Premise: "What's the Opposite Opinion to My Chosen Punch–Premise?"
Next, form the setup–premise for each punch–premise. This is an easy step—just find the opposite, positive, opinion to that of your punch–premise's negative opinion. Ask the step's question:

Q: What's the opposite opinion to my chosen punch–premise?
A: Setup–premises: a. My relationship with my mother was very good.
b. My father was brilliant.
c. My brother made things better.
d. Our family vacations were pleasant.

E. Choose a Setup–Premise and Write a List of Setups: "What are Some Examples or Statements That Express My Setup–Premise?"
Frank has the most issues with his mother, so he chose:

Setup–premise: My *relationship with my mother was very good.*

Now he can start writing setups by thinking of examples and statements that express the setup–premise. It's important to notice that since the opinion in the setup–premise is often *untrue*, it requires an imagination to answer this step's question. Be creative and make up some examples and statements as if the setup–premise were real. Begin by answering the step's question:

Q: What are some examples or statements that express my setup–premise (*my relationship with my mother was very good.*)?
A: Setups: a. "I call my mom all the time—
b. "I send my mom flowers on every holiday—
c. "I had problems with my mom growing up, but now that I'm older—
d. "Thinking about my mother always makes me smile—

All these setups are consistent with the setup–premise that *my relationship with my mother was very good.*

When you do this step, remember not to put too much information in a setup, because you can get lost in all the assumptions associated with it. Keep it as short as you can; include all of the information you need, but no more.

Having successfully finished the Joke Map, it's time to go onto the next phase of the Joke Prospector—the Joke Mine. Now we can start digging into one of Frank's setups to find punches for them.

The Joke Mine: From Setup to Punch

Since the Joke Mine was covered in Chapter 2, we'll just take a quick tour here to demonstrate its relationship to the Joke Map.

1. SELECT A SETUP, THEN LIST THE ASSUMPTIONS: "WHAT AM I ASSUMING ABOUT THIS STATEMENT?"
Frank chose, "I call my mom all the time—."

Q: What am I assuming about this statement?

> Assumptions: a. *Call* means to telephone her.
> b. They're pleasant calls.
> c. She's my natural mother.

(When writing a joke of your own, you could come up with a punch anywhere along the passage. If you do, write it down.)

2. PICK A TARGET ASSUMPTION, AND IDENTIFY THE CONNECTOR: "WHAT IS THE THING THAT CAUSED ME TO MAKE THIS TARGET ASSUMPTION?"
Frank chose assumption (a) as the target assumption, since it's the most obvious one.

> Target assumption: *Call means to telephone her.*

He uncovered the connector by asking this step's question:

Q: What is the thing that caused me to make this target assumption?

> Connector: *The word* call

44

3. List Some Reinterpretations for the Connector: "Other than the target, what other interpretations are there for my connector?"
Asking this step's question, Frank came up with:

> Reinterpretations: a. *Call* means calling out someone's name.
>   b. *Call* means a referee making a call or decision.
>   c. *Call* means name-calling.

4. Choose a Reinterpretation, and Compose a 2nd Story: "Relative to the setup, what specific situation could explain my reinterpretation?"
Of the three possibilities, Frank chose:

> Reinterpretation: Call *means name-calling.*

Notice how the reinterpretation, *I call my mother names*, supports our punch–premise, *My relationship with my mother was very bad.* Ask this step's question:

Q: Relative to the setup, what specific situation explains my reinterpretation?
A: Calling my mother bad names would explain why my relationship with her is bad.

Now, to form the 2nd story, get a few more details about *what* bad names you call her.

Q: What kind of bad things do I say when I call her?

> I tell her she's a bitch and a drunk and yell at her about how she used to lock me in the closet and how she's ruined my life.

Well, that's certainly clearer. Kind of brutal, but not everyone has a nice relationship with their parents.

5. Write a Punch That Expresses the 2nd Story: "In addition to the setup, what information is needed to communicate my 2nd story clearly?"
Knowing what the joke is about, the task now is to distill the 2nd story down to a concise punch. When you're doing this, you might have

to ask many questions until you find the phrasing that tickles your funny bone. Remember, brevity is the key.

Q: In addition to the setup, what information is needed to communicate my 2nd story clearly?

> I call my mother all the time—but in polite company, I can't tell you what I call her.

There it is. A joke written without waiting around for the muse, by simply following all the steps of the Joke Prospector from the Joke Map through the Joke Mine. In essence, the results of those steps are:

Topic:	*My family*
Punch–premise:	*My relationship with my mother was very bad.*
Setup–premise:	*My relationship with my mother was very good.*

Diagram 12 illustrates the progression from topic to punch. Again, notice how the punch–premise and the punch are related by the negative opinion, and how the setup–premise and the setup share the same opinion.

Diagram 12
I call my mom all the time—

Setup

> **Target Assumption:** Call *means to telephone her.*
>
> **Connector:** *the word* call.
>
> **Reinterpretation:** Call *means name-calling.*
>
> **2nd Story:** *I tell her she's a bitch and a drunk and yell at her about how she used to lock me in the closet and how she's ruined my life.*
>
> but in polite company, I can't tell you what I call her.

Punch

Joke Map Options: Plotting Another Course

The Joke Prospector system offers many options. If you're not pleased with your jokes, it's easy to change your direction. Since we've already discussed the Joke Mine's options in Chapter 2, I'll only list the options for the Joke Map:

Go Back to Step E: Choose a Different Setup–Premise   A great way to construct a whole routine is to choose another setup–premise and write some more setups. Then, with those setups, reenter the Joke Mine.

Go Back to Step C: Create More Punch–Premises   It's amazing how many possible punch–premises each topic has. If you finish writing some, write some more. Every item on your association list can be used to create a punch–premise. And from my own experience, I've found that an association list is almost limitless.

Go Back to Step B: Pick Another Topic   Once you've thoroughly explored a particular topic, go to the top of the Joke Map and pick another one. The advantage of the Joke Prospector system is that it opens up the possibility of writing about almost anything.

Go Back to Step A: List More Topics   When you've run out of topics, start searching for other things that you have issues with or negative thoughts or feelings about. Remember, comedy is a playful means of dealing with painful things. The more horrific a concept, the better it usually is for comedy.

Customization

The Joke Prospector is the only step-by-step system for writing jokes. The goal of the Joke Map is to help you with the process of selecting a topic in order to write setups. Then, with those setups, you can dig into the Joke Mine to find punches. Even though this is systematic, it doesn't require you to follow the steps verbatim. Feel free to alter these ideas in any fashion that suits you and your style.

I have one student, Bill Fulco, who's customized the whole system. He creates his punch–premise, then jumps to the end of the Joke Mine and writes punches. After that, he goes back to the Joke Map, notes the setup–premise, and writes setups for his punches. This works for him. Do what works for you.

Now it's time to practice writing jokes using the Joke Prospector. The following form includes the steps of the Joke Map which will guide you in writing setups. To write punches for your setups, you'll need to refer to the Joke Mine form (page 32). Use a separate sheet of paper so you can freely explore all options. And as you do, remember your options. Joke writing is a journey, not a destination.

Practicing the Joke Prospector
The Joke Map

A. List Some Topics *(single subject—something wrong—no opinion)*:
"What are some things I consider wrong that I'm interested in talking about?"

Topics: _____

B. Select One Topic and Make an Association List: "What are all the things I can think of that relate to my topic?"

Topic: _____

List: _____

C. Create Several Punch–premises *(smaller aspect—negative opinion—no example)*:
"What negative opinions do I have about some smaller aspects of my topic?"

Punch–Premises: _____

D. For Each Punch–premise Form a Setup–premise *(opposite opinion)*:
"What's the opposite opinion to my chosen punch–premise?"

Setup–Premises: _____

E. Choose a Setup–premise and Write a List of Setups: "What are some examples or statements that express my setup–premise?"

Setup–premise: _____

Setups: _____

Using your own setups go to Practicing the Joke Mine (see page 32)

4

From Funny to Funnier
Improving and Polishing Your Gems

A famous writer once said, "There is no writing, only rewriting." That may be extreme, but the point is well-taken. Once you have a first draft, there are many things you can do to improve it. Sometimes you hit the nail on the head with your first shot. But more often than not, when you go about polishing your jokes you'll discover there are many possible versions depending on which technique you employ.

In this chapter, you'll learn some basic guidelines for sharpening your jokes as well as a few techniques for expanding them. These methods come from my own experience as a working comic and from the tried-and-true writing techniques of successful comedians I've worked with over the years. But remember, these are *not* laws or rules—they're guidelines. In the end, what works for you is what counts, so use these helpful ideas as you see fit.

One word of advice: Don't worry about polishing and improving your material *while* you're coming up with it. Creating and editing are two very different and mutually exclusive functions. When you're writing new jokes, write quickly and move on. Later, come back to polish the rough gems you've dug up. Otherwise, you'll kill your momentum and leave a lot of tunnels unexplored. Also, you'll often find that when you come back to a joke a day or so later, you have a fresh perspective and new ideas. So write first, improve later.

Economy

As Shakespeare said, "Brevity is levity." Nothing kills a good joke more certainly than smothering it with an avalanche of unnecessary words and information. I talked a little about this subject when you were first learning to write a punch.

50

A student of mine, Terry R. Jackson, brought a very funny but over-written joke to class. It went like this:

I just went through a long and messy separation, which ended in a divorce from my wife. So, after all that, I went on a vacation to Denmark because I was having a sex change. The sex change was from not very often to nothing at all.

This central idea of this joke is good, but it includes a lot of information about the 2nd story that the audience doesn't need to know in order to get the punch. In fact, it becomes confusing when they have to sift through all those unnecessary details to identify which assumption is being shattered.

As a general rule, the audience should *respond* to your jokes, not *think* about them. This doesn't mean you shouldn't write intelligent jokes. It means that a joke, even if it's a novel idea, should be so understandable that the audience doesn't have to figure out what you're talking about.

Comedy has its own conservation of energy law: *Energy spent by the audience thinking is energy taken away from laughing.* That's why it's important to give them no more information to process than absolutely necessary.

Your setup should include just enough information to establish your target assumption, and even that should be as concise as possible. Then give the audience a punch—a reinterpretation that shatters your target assumption. Nothing more is needed.

I pointed all this out to Terry and advised him to reread the section in his class workbook on improving material. The following week, he brought back this version of his joke:

After my divorce, I had a sex change—from very seldom to not at all.

That's an excellently constructed joke. Neither more nor less is needed. It gets a bigger laugh than the original version, yet requires a smaller time investment for the payoff. The less time it takes to get a laugh, the more *laughs per minute*, LPMs, you get. Economy is an important technique for achieving high LPMs.

End the Punch with the Reveal

Within every punch there's a pivotal word, phrase, or action that presents the reinterpretation, which in turn shatters the target assumption with the intent of making the audience laugh. From the audience's perspective, this pivotal word, phrase, or action is hidden until the punch exposes it, which is why I call this technique the *reveal*.

To effectively construct a joke, make sure your reveal appears at the very end of the punch. A properly placed reveal is a very important factor, because it determines when the audience laughs. If the reveal is positioned too early in your punch, the audience will begin to laugh, you will continue to talk, and they will stop laughing to hear what you have to say.

One night at the Comedy Store in Hollywood, I watched a comic train an audience to stop laughing. In the beginning the audience laughed at his jokes, but since his reveals were too early in his punch he would yell over the laughter to finish his joke. Of course the audience quickly learned to be quiet. This is not what you want to teach your audience. After the tenth joke, the audience had stopped laughing, but were politely smiling and still enjoying his show. However, since he wasn't getting laughs he became agitated and began blaming them for being a bad audience. Now they stopped smiling. This was partly the result of the comic not understanding the technique of placing his reveals at the end of his punch. There are two basic mistakes comics tend to make in this area.

Unnecessary Words Are Said or Actions Are Done After the Reveal

Talking past the reveal is one of the most common and irritating errors. It usually occurs because the comic inserts mindless prattle beyond the point where the joke gets a laugh. For example, take this joke written by a gay student, Robert A. Smith:

> Do you know why gays are such good dressers? You try spending twenty years in the closet and see what happens to you.

And see what happens to you has nothing to do with the joke and should be eliminated. Here's how Robert correctly phrased the joke, ending with the reveal:

> Do you know why gays are such good dressers? You try spending twenty years in the closet.

Closet is the reveal, so anything beyond that would only defuse the joke's power.

The Reveal Gets Mixed Up
with Other Important Information

It's imperative to identify the reveal; otherwise it may get mixed up with less important information needed to make the joke work. Here's an example:

> They have this new Fire and Theft Insurance. But only if your house is robbed while it's burning do they pay.

Can you see how to make this joke better? It ends with *do they pay*, which is an important phrase, but not as important as the reveal, *robbed while it's burning*. Here's a version with more effective wording:

> They have this new Fire and Theft Insurance. But they only pay if your house is robbed *while* it's burning.

After comparing these two versions, you can see that placing the reveal at the end of the punch makes for a more potent joke. Of course, you won't always be able to get the reveal into a single word or quick phrase at the very end of a joke, either because of the restraints of sentence structure or because you have to get certain information out in a particular way. Do your best to get it as near to the end of the punch as possible while still allowing for normal speech.

Now that you know about this technique, watch the stand-up comedy shows on TV and count how many times even professional comics muck up their own jokes with an improperly placed reveal. Then revel in the knowledge that you know how to end your punches correctly.

Use Words or Phrases with Hard Consonants

The hard consonant sounds, especially *K* sounds, which include hard *C*, *Qu*, and, to a lesser extent, *T*, *P*, hard *G*, *D*, and *B*, tend to make words sound funnier. Using words with these hard consonants instead of synonyms with softer sounds really helps improve a joke.

Most comics who've been in the business long enough will tell you that it happens to be true:

"Words with a *K* in them are funny."—Neil Simon

"An egg is funny, an orange is not."—Fred Allen

For instance, in this version of a joke by Margaret Smith, I've replaced a couple of hard-consonant words with softer ones:

> I hate singles bars. Guys come up to me and say, 'Hey, sweetie, can I buy you a drink?' I say, 'No, but I'll take the three dollars.'

Now check out the original version with the hard consonant words that Margaret chose. Read it out loud so you can really hear the difference.

> I hate singles bars. Guys come up to me and say, 'Hey, *cupcake*, can I buy you a drink?' I say, 'No, but I'll take the three *bucks*.'

This version of the joke *sounds* funnier. The words *cupcake* and *bucks* just have more punch than *sweetie* and *dollars*.

Make it a habit to search for words with hard consonants and test this out for yourself.

Use Rhythms of Three

This trick is passed around among comics as some mystical rule for making things funny, but ask them why so many jokes include a series of three and they can't tell you.

You, however, *do* know why. A pattern is a simple way to get people to make an assumption because they assume the pattern will continue. And what is the smallest number of beats needed to set up a pattern? You've got it—two. Two beats set up the pattern and the assumption, and the third beat breaks the pattern, shattering the assumption. Classic joke structure.

Always be on the lookout for a series of three, because it is a cue—a perfect opportunity to stick in a joke. Here are a few examples:

> They have these dresses in small, medium, and tent.
>
> I'm very sensitive. When I see a beautiful woman, I want to cry . . . write poetry . . . jump on her.
>
> The FDA sets allowable levels of rat feces in breakfast cereals. Maybe they should change that ad to Snap, Crackle, and Poop.

Stick to Common Knowledge

If they don't understand what you're talking about, they won't laugh. When a certain word or reference is crucial to the understanding of a joke, you must consider whether it's familiar to your audience. Sometimes you'll need to use a more familiar alternative.

For example, take this joke in which Woody Allen talks about his rabbi:

> He opened a discotheque with his colleagues. Topless rabbis. No skullcaps.

Woody Allen knows that the little round caps Jewish men wear are called yarmulkes, but since he is also aware that many people in his audience won't know that word, he uses the term *skullcap*, which is self-explanatory.

If there's a reference or information that's crucial to your joke that is not in the common realm of knowledge and has no convenient alternative, explain the reference or state the information in the setup. Sadly, once in a while you'll have to drop a joke altogether because explaining the reference kills the comedy or gives away the punch. For example, when I was in college, this line was going around:

> I took this great LSD, and I saw God.

At the time it was very hip to take a philosophy class, so it was common knowledge around campus that the philosopher Friedrich Nietzsche was renowned for having said, "God is dead." I used that information to form this comeback line:

> I took some even better LSD, and I saw Nietzsche.

At parties around the school this joke got big laughs. But when I started performing and delivered this same joke at the Comedy Store in Hollywood, not only did the audience *not* laugh, they stared at me with the expression of the RCA Victor dog. And no matter how I tried to explain who Nietzsche was, the joke never worked.

If they don't have the knowledge and explaining it doesn't work, they won't get the joke, and you'll find yourself saying, "I guess you had to be there."

Quote Whenever Possible

In a sense, this falls under one of the primary rules for all good fiction writing—show, don't tell. For our purposes, it means when writing out a joke that involves a scene or a bit of dialogue, quote yourself as well as any characters. This sets the stage for you to play yourself and *become* the character in the scene.

Here's an example written by a student, Davy-O. He begins by lighting a cigarette.

My girlfriend asked me, "How do you know when it's time to smoke?" I said, "Well, that would be whenever you start talking."

Notice the attributions *asked* and *said* came before the quote. This is the way it should be done. Putting the attribution verb in the middle of the quote would interrupt the flow and confuse the audience about who's speaking.

Quoting yourself and the characters in your jokes brings the scene into the present, greatly adds to the reality of the performance with personal interactions, and provides opportunities to find more jokes.

In General, Avoid Puns

Puns are an old, somewhat outdated style of comedy. In vaudeville, they were an accepted form of humor. If you read the old routines, you'll often find jokes like this one:

I goosed a ghost and got a handful of sheet.

Admittedly, puns can be fun, especially really bad ones like this:

The boarding house blew up, and the roomers were flying.

But while they might be useful for annoying your friends, puns in professional comedy almost invariably produce groans. That's probably because a good joke, like a good magic trick, is only effective if the audience doesn't see how it's done. No form of joke displays its inner workings more overtly than a pun. To make matters worse, someone doing a pun always seems to be saying, "Hey, look how clever I am with words." I don't know about you, but my usual reaction to that attitude is an immediate and passionate desire to run away from the punster.

For all these reasons, puns generally don't make very good jokes, with three occasional exceptions:

1. The pun that's so genuinely clever it's interesting to hear. Like this one, for instance: "Time flies like an arrow. Fruit flies like a banana." It means nothing, but it engages your brain anyway. Sometimes that's enough.

2. The pun has two phrases related by something more meaningful than sound alone, so that it makes some kind of comment. For example: "I'm for term limits in politics. Some of our senators have been in this town so long, they date all the way back to Washington, B.C." This pun underscores a point and is worth a shot at least.

3. You use a pun because you *want* to get a groan. Why? You have a line ready as a comeback. For instance, in San Diego, I watched a street juggler use a pun to intentionally provoke a groan just so he could respond with this put down:

Look, if you had any taste you wouldn't be here in the first place.

The laugh he got with the comeback made it worth going through the groan. But only use this technique once per show.

I've had students oppose my view of puns, saying, "Well, it's better to get a groan than no response at all." It's up to you, of course, but be clear about your goals. If you want to get groans, then by all means pun it up. If you're aiming for a five LPM average show, though, strive for that goal until you achieve it. Don't cop out for a measly groan.

Make Your Characters Specific and Get Personal

Making the characters in your jokes real and specific greatly enhances the jokes' effectiveness. Lines such as "These two guys went into a bar . . . " have been out of style for years. The audience wants to know who those two guys are. Giving them that information creates what fiction writers call *verisimilitude*, the quality of a story seeming more lifelike and believable because of little added details.

Refer to the characters in your jokes as friends or relatives rather than nebulous persons, or use actual public figures. Here's an example of this concept in a joke from Mike Binder:

My parents sent my brother through law school. He graduated. Now he's suing them for wasting seven years of his life.

This joke could have been about "*some* parents who sent *their* kid through law school," but Mike Binder made it about *his* parents and *his* brother. It doesn't matter if he has a brother or not because comics often make up fictional siblings and relatives to personalize their jokes.

Here's an example of improving a joke by using a real person the audience knows something about.

Cher has a tattoo of a butterfly on her breast. It's kinda pretty now, but when she's eighty it's gonna look like a big ol' bat.

This is actually an old joke that usually begins with, "I saw this young woman . . . ." Telling it about Cher makes it seem much more realistic and even a little less jokey.

Another way to personalize your material is to make the joke about a particular member of your audience. For example, you could tell a joke about some guy you know who wears powerful eyeglasses, but it's a lot more fun to goof with someone in the crowd who's actually wearing glasses:

(Take glasses off man in audience.) Oh my, you could use these to burn ants. (Put them on yourself.) Wow, I can see the bones in my hand. (To woman sitting nearby.) Nice slip, ma'am. (Hand glasses back.) Here are your glasses back, Mr. Hubble.

A routine like this engages the audience in what you're doing a thousand percent more and usually comes off as improvisational, creating the illusion that you're even more brilliant than you really are.

Localize Your References

On a similar note, insert the names of local landmarks, neighboring cities, regional hotels, stores, and restaurants into your jokes. It isn't as difficult as you might think, and it can really improve the response you'll receive.

If you have a joke that involves a restaurant, learn the name of a well-known local eatery. Then instead of saying, "I was at this restaurant the other day . . . ," you can say, "I was just at Joe's Diner." If you're in the South and have a joke about being in a supermarket, say, "I was in the Piggly Wiggly," not, "I was at this market . . . ."

Every town has an area or some nearby town that people look down on. Find out what it is and refer to it. Make it the place that an unlikable character in one of your jokes comes from. The audience will love you for it.

For example, I live in Los Angeles, and here we make fun of Bakersfield. In Bakersfield, they make fun of . . . Bakersfield.

If you have a joke about a rough bar, ask around for the name of a local dive that fits the bill.

> I walked into [insert name of tough local bar]—they've got some poor guy on the floor, and they're pounding the snot out of him. I asked the bartender, "Why don't you call a cop?" He says, "Are you crazy? After the beating they just gave that one?"

Something magical happens when an audience sees their home town immortalized in your show. This technique works so well, in fact, that some comics actually pooh-pooh it for being too easy to pull off. I say it's just doing your homework.

Adapt Your Jokes to Topical Events

There's an old joke about an American tourist in Paris who gets propositioned on the street by a prostitute while his wife is inside a shop. The prostitute offers her services for a hundred francs, and the man gets rid of her by saying he only has five francs on him. A little later that evening, he comes around a corner with his wife and runs into the same prostitute. She takes one glance at the wife and says, "There. See what you get for five francs?"

It's a cute old joke that gets a nice laugh, but this could get a much better laugh by making it about Bill and Hillary Clinton on a diplomatic visit to Moscow. Suddenly, it's a topical joke with whole new dimensions. Tying your old jokes in with current news stories helps make your material sound fresh and up to date.

Here's a little tip: Have some jokes and routines handy for all of the special calendar days, such as Christmas, Halloween, Secretary's Day, and so on. You can do these "topical" jokes year after year, and they'll never get old.

Will Durst, who lives in the Bay Area, can always call on this joke:

> In San Francisco, Halloween is redundant.

A Mexican-born student, Maria G. Martinez, studied with me for several years. Every Christmas she'll pull out this ditty:

> Here in America, you have so many Santa Claus. But in Mexico we have no Santa Claus—they are all *here* looking for work.

Using Grammatically Incorrect Language Is Okay

People don't talk like they write, so you should write like they talk. Proper grammar and syntax have nothing to do with making a joke funny. In fact, stiffly worded jokes seldom flow as well as jokes written with the flaws and rhythms of everyday speech.

Here's part of a routine on sponge fishermen by Tom McTigue:

> Old guys sit around in the twilight of their lives swapping sponge tales: "He was huge! Biggest sponge you ever seen! Son of a bitch damn near absorbed me! Huge! Had Comet all over him!"

In these faulty, fractured, incomplete sentences, Tom has captured the natural speech of an old unschooled fisherman. If the idiom of your character includes terrible English, use it. Correcting the grammar would only detract from the joke.

Feel Free to Make up Words

Comedic license permits comedians to muck around with language for the purpose of making jokes. For instance, Robin Williams does this take on divorce:

> Divorce comes from the old Latin word *divorcerum*, meaning "having your genitals torn out through your wallet."

Of course, *divorcerum* is not really a Latin word, but it sounds funny and fits the joke. In comedy, that's enough.

You should feel completely free to play around with language. Don't worry about the rules you learned in school. Language is your comedic clay—mash and twist it any way you think will shape your joke into something really funny.

Sometimes a Sight Gag Is Better

Sometimes seeing a joke is funnier than hearing it. For example, a student of mine, Alan Bockal, does this joke:

> So look for me at your local freeway off-ramp. I'll be the one holding the sign that says: (*He shows a cardboard sign that reads*: MARRIED A JEWISH GIRL—WILL WORK FOR SEX.)

Alan could have just said that joke, but it works much better when he stands there holding the sign like a jobless person on a freeway off-ramp.

Comedian and food fan Kevin James has an entire routine about how tiny a Geo Metro feels when he sits in it. He could, of course, just tell the audience that the car fits like a jacket, but instead he pretends to be in the car, holding a steering wheel that appears to be the size of a donut and hanging his elbows out of both windows. The sight of his obvious discomfort is much funnier than any description could ever be.

Don't be afraid to try acting out scenes instead of talking about them. Be careful about using props, though. Not because it's cheating or hackish (as some comics mistakenly believe), but because, practically speaking, schlepping a lot of props from gig to gig can get to be a real drag. If the joke really needs it, and you don't mind carrying it around, there's absolutely nothing wrong with using a prop.

Tag Your Jokes

Tagging a joke is a comic's slang for adding another punch to a completed joke. Getting two or more laughs from your initial setup increases your overall LPMs.

Tags are the road to success. If all you do is setup and punch, 95 to 99 percent of you're stage time is spent on the setups. That means 95 to 99 percent of your time is spent not being funny. But if you're tagging all your setups with multiple punches, you increase your LPMs, hence the percentage of time you spend being funny. If you think of a setup as an investment of time with the laugh as your payoff, then tagging a joke is like getting paid again and again for the same investment. Following are the three techniques for tagging a joke.

1. USE THE ORIGINAL TARGET ASSUMPTION

Here's a joke by my good friend Allan Murray with two tags built on the same target assumption as the original punch:

> I was into Buddhism for a while, until I saw a statue of Buddha. It's hard to get behind a god who looks like Curly from the Three Stooges. [end of punch] (*Speaking as Buddha, patting his big fat belly*) "Hey, I'm starving. Where's that buffet?" [first tag] (*Belches, as Buddha*) "Brrrrp, excuse me." [second tag]

The original punch and both tags are based on the target assumption that *a god must be perfect*. That assumption is shattered by the original punch, which portrays the Buddha as "looking like Curly from the Three Stooges." Then the first tag shatters that same assumption by implying that he's a glutton, and the second tag by demonstrating that he's crude.

2. BASE THE TAG ON A DIFFERENT 1ST STORY ASSUMPTION

Remember the exercise in the Joke Mine where you wrote a punch for the setup, "For Father's Day, I took my father out—"? Here's an example of a punch with a tag that shatters a different 1st story assumption.

> For Father's day I took my father out—permanently. [punch] I couldn't stand the way he said Mass. [tag]

The initial punch shatters the assumption that *took out* means *taking his father to some sort of celebration dinner*, with the reinterpretation that *took out* means *killed his father*. Then notice how the tag shatters another 1st story assumption, that *father* means *biological father* with the reinterpretation that *father* means *priest*. A punch and a tag shattering two different assumptions from the same 1st story.

You can also use the Joke Mine to write tags for your punches. After you've written a punch, simply go back and look at your original list of assumptions. If you find another one you can shatter without conflicting with the original joke, you've got yourself a tag.

3. A NEW ASSUMPTION CREATED BY THE 2ND STORY

With every new punch comes a 2nd story filled with numerous assumptions. Using the same setup, here's another punch, but this time with a tag that shatters an assumption from the 2nd story:

> For Father's Day, I took my father out—it only took seven shots. [punch] I could always drink him under the table. [tag]

Again, recognize how the initial punch shatters the target assumption, that *took out* means *celebration dinner*, with the reinterpretation that *took out* means *he killed his father*. Then notice how the punch, "it only took seven shots," creates a 2nd story with a new target assumption, that *shots* means *gun shots*, which is shattered by the tag's reinterpretation that *shots* means *shots of liquor*. Remember, every punch or tag carries with it a 2nd story filled with new assumptions ripe for a tag.

The Joke Mine can also be helpful for writing tags by treating every punch or tag as a new setup. Ask yourself what new assumptions you're making about the punch or tag, and go down the list of questions in the Joke Mine until you dig up with another punch.

Improving your material may seem like a lot of work at first, but once you get into it you'll realize it's just as creative a process as writing a first draft. Fine-tuning your jokes can make the difference between getting a chuckle or a really big laugh. Stick with it, and you'll find the increased number and volume of laughs well worth the effort.

5

Assembling a Routine

Now that you understand how to use the Joke Prospector to write enough jokes for an entire routine, what do you do with jokes that come from different premises, are in random order, or are disconnected thoughts? This chapter will teach you how to string your jokes together to build a coherent routine.

SECRET #7:

MAINTAIN A JOKE AND ROUTINE FILE.

A joke file is a means of organizing and recording your material. It usually consists of cards stored in an index box or a comparable computer program. When you write a joke you consider a keeper, file it two or three times based on the subjects it addresses. Take this joke:

> All my friends say I'm paranoid. Well, I didn't *actually* hear them say it.

I'd file this under: *paranoia, psychology,* and *friends.* This way, you'll be able to find it if you're working on a bit involving any of these related topics. Also, as you assemble more routines, you can use this same filing system for keeping them organized as well.

When I began writing jokes I would write ten jokes a day for four days, then on the fifth day, clean up the best ones and file them. I suggest you do this same practice because it will give you a daily goal to reach. If you are able to write one hysterical joke a week, at the end of a year you will have 52 hilarious jokes.

My close friend Tim Simpson has been maintaining a joke file in his computer for nearly ten years. He recently reported to me that he has accumulated more than 15,000 original jokes and funny concepts. Whenever anyone asks him to write on a particular subject, he simply searches his database, retrieves a multitude of jokes, and begins working on a job that's already half finished.

The Routine Builder is a procedure to help you assemble your jokes into a routine. Different people can take the same jokes and end up forming very different routines, so the Routine Builder is designed to allow for personal preferences. Always feel free to customize the Routine Builder and experiment until you find your own style of arranging jokes. If any of these steps seem out of order or useless to you, rearrange or skip them. Here we go:

Routine Builder
1. Put each joke on a separate index card
2. Organize the jokes into categories
3. Arrange jokes so one thought leads to the next
4. Rewrite, rewrite, rewrite

We'll go though the steps, one by one, to demonstrate how this method takes you from a disorganized group of jokes to a coherent routine. Let's begin with the jokes below I wrote about the post office. I want you to take special notice of the fact that not all the jokes I come up with are produced by going through all of the steps of the Joke Prospector. Some of them are ideas that just come to me, others are switches of old jokes, still others began as random setups that didn't come from a setup–premise, and so on. Sometimes setups or jokes occur to me while I'm doing one of the steps, or I'll go through the steps and won't come up with anything at all, only to wake up the next morning with jokes coming to mind faster than I can write them down. Some jokes even come from other people. It doesn't matter how it happens. As long as the eventual outcome is the same—good jokes. Here they are:

1. The post office has a logo of an eagle streaking through the sky. Yeah, right. It should be a slug taking a nap.
2. I don't mind long lines if at the end I get to ride the Matterhorn.
3. When the line got really long, I yelled, "The line is getting long. Can you close one of the windows?" And they did.
4. The postal workers are actually very efficient—with guns.
   Tag: After all, their motto is "Neither snow, nor rain, etc. shall keep them from their *rounds*."
5. I don't understand why so many postal workers get killed by

other postal workers. You'd think they'd be killed by disgruntled customers.

6. If the post office had to operate like a real business, it'd be about as successful as a steak house in India.

7. The post office has stamps of famous people like Marilyn Monroe, Martin Luther King—where's the commemorative series celebrating Charles Manson?

8. Stamps only depict old-fashioned inventions like the cotton gin or the steam engine. What about the important modern inventions like breast implants?

   Tag 1: Hey, I'd become a collector.

   Tag 2: They could release them in pairs.

   Tag 3: Of course, guys would lick them on both sides.

9. *Postal service* is an oxymoron.

10. I was checking out one of those mug shots of this particularly tough, nasty looking, lowlife—it was the employee of the month.

11. After hearing my opinions, a postal worker said to me, "You shouldn't insult postal workers." I said, "Why not?" And he said, "Because we know where you live." Then I shot back, "Even if you did come after me, you'd just show up at the wrong house."

12. The people who design the stamps have never done one honoring the post office. Are they afraid people will spit on the wrong side?

These jokes are the starting point. You may like some of them and dislike others, but remember, they're meant to be said, not read. Besides, we still have a long way to go before these jokes are ready to be performed. The challenge is to arrange them into a coherent routine using the four steps.

1. Put Each Joke on a Separate Index Card

Put each joke on a separate three-by-five- or four-by-six-inch index card or separate line on your computer screen. If the joke has an indelibly linked tag or tags, you can place them all on the same card or next line on the screen because their order is already set. If you've been keeping a joke file, your jokes should already be on index cards or in some sort of filing system on your computer. If you're going to do stand-up comedy for a living, you'll constantly be coming up with ideas and writing jokes, so you might as well develop the habit of keeping your jokes organized.

2. Organize the Jokes into Categories

Organize your jokes into categories by placing the cards into like groupings. If you've written your jokes using the Joke Prospector, they will often organize themselves into categories based the subject of your premises—but not necessarily. Sometimes a joke from one premise will fit better with jokes from another category. Joke writing isn't a linear science; it's erratic and unpredictable. So this step requires that you take the time to evaluate your jokes and cluster them in related categories.

Below are my post office jokes separated into categories and accompanied by a little explanation. There are no rules about how they should be organized, so don't try to do it perfectly. You can always change the order around later.

You may disagree with how I've categorized these jokes. That's a good sign. If you have an opinion about how this should by done, then you're getting the hang of it.

I'm placing jokes 1, 6, and 9 together in the *service* category because they all reflect, in one form or another, the post office's poor record for service.

Service

1. The post office has a logo of an eagle streaking through the sky. Yeah, right. It should be a slug taking a nap.
6. If the post office had to operate like a real business, it'd be about as successful as a steak house in India.
9. *Postal service* is an oxymoron.

Jokes 2 and 3 are both about post office *lines*.

Lines

2. I don't mind long lines if at the end I get to ride the Matterhorn.

3. When the line got really long, I yelled, "The line is getting long. Can you close one of the windows?" And they did.

Jokes 4, 5, 10, and 11 all have the theme of *postal workers*.

Postal Workers

4. The postal workers are actually very efficient—with guns.
Tag: After all, their motto is "Neither snow, nor rain, etc. shall keep them from their *rounds*."
5. I don't understand why so many postal workers get killed by other postal workers. You'd think they'd be killed by disgruntled customers.
10. I was checking out one of those mug shots of this particularly tough, nasty looking, lowlife—it was the employee of the month.
11. After hearing my opinions, a postal worker said to me, "You shouldn't insult postal workers." I said, "Why not?" And he said, "Because we know where you live." Then I shot back, "Even if you did come after me, you'd just show up at the wrong house."

And jokes 7, 8, and 12 are all about *stamps*.

Stamps

7. The post office has stamps of famous people like Marilyn Monroe, Martin Luther King—where's the commemorative series celebrating Charles Manson?
8. Stamps only depict old-fashioned inventions, like the cotton gin or the steam engine. What about the important modern inventions, like breast implants?
Tag 1: Hey, I'd become a collector.
Tag 2: They could release them in pairs.
Tag 3: Of course, guys would lick them on both sides.
12. The people who design the stamps have never done one honoring the post office. Are they afraid people will spit on the wrong side?

Getting the hang of it? It's really simple. If the jokes seem to fit together, put them in the same category. In this case we didn't run into any conflict, but sometimes you'll have a joke that fits into several categories. When that occurs, put it in the group you think it fits best. You can always rearrange it later.

3. Arrange Jokes So One Thought Leads to the Next

When you have all your jokes on cards and they're sorted into categories, it's time to arrange the pieces of this puzzle into a connected series of thoughts. Again, there's no right way to do this. If you're the kind of person who jumps from one thought to the next, then order the jokes to fit that flighty line of thought. If your thoughts follow a logical path, then connect the jokes so it seems as if the idea of one joke makes you think of the subject of the next. Remember, this is personal. What you're trying to do is to arrange the jokes to express *your* funny thoughts about the topic.

To begin the routine, it seems logical to me to start by complaining about the *service*, so I'll put the service group first, consisting of jokes 1, 6, and 9.

Service

The post office has a logo of an eagle streaking through the sky. Yeah, right. It should be a slug taking a nap. If the post office had to operate like a real business, it'd be about as successful as a steak house in India. *Postal service* is an oxymoron.

Next, I'll put in the category about lines. Since it's a form of complaining about the service, it would logically follow. Now we've added jokes 2 and 3 to the routine.

Lines

I don't mind long lines if at the end I get to ride the Matterhorn. When the line got really long, I yelled, "The line is getting long. Can you close one of the windows?" And they did.

These two jokes seem to work okay together, though I'm still not crazy about the Matterhorn joke. But I'll fix it later.

I predicted that I'm going to end this routine with the *stamp* jokes, so there's only the *postal workers* jokes 4, 5, 10, and 11 to add as the next part of this routine. Besides, the second joke in the *lines* category is about a postal worker closing a window, which naturally brings up the subject of postal workers.

Postal Workers

The postal workers are actually very efficient—with guns. After all, their motto is "Neither snow, nor rain, etc. shall keep them from their *rounds.*" I don't understand why so many postal workers get killed by other postal workers. You'd think they'd be killed by disgruntled customers. I was checking out one of those mug shots of this particularly tough, nasty looking, lowlife—it was the employee of the month. After hearing my opinions, a postal worker said to me, "You shouldn't insult postal workers." I said, "Why not?" And he said, "Because we know where you live." Then I shot back, "Even if you did come after me, you'd just show up at the wrong house."

The final category, *stamps*, consists of jokes 7, 8, and 12. I think the breast implant joke and its tags are the funniest, so I'll go ahead and put them last. Also, the Charles Manson joke doesn't bring up the subject of stamps very well, so I'm going to start this series of jokes with the "tribute to the post office." Here's my shot at it.

Stamps

The people who design the stamps have never done one honoring the post office. Are they afraid people will spit on the wrong side? The post office has stamps of famous people like Marilyn Monroe, Martin Luther King—where's the commemorative series celebrating Charles Manson? Stamps only depict old-fashioned inventions like the cotton gin or the steam engine. What about the important modern inventions, like breast implants? Hey, I'd become a collector. They could release them in pairs. Of course, guys would lick them on both sides.

Actually, this routine seems to flow rather nicely. Many routines I've put together in the past had a number of jokes in a category I call *miscellaneous*, which includes all the jokes I don't know where to place. This particular routine was written primarily from the Joke Prospector, so it tends to be more systematic because of the logical progression laid out by that method. But what if you've been collecting jokes on the same subject for a year? When you attempt to organize them into a routine, they won't all fit into a nicely ordered series of thoughts.

Don't toss those jokes out; in the next step you can often find a spot for them.

4. *Rewrite, Rewrite, Rewrite*

This final step is much more complex than the previous three steps put together. You'll need to experiment with wording, editing, and reordering to make the jokes flow as an entire routine. When you're rewriting, *read the jokes out loud.* You'll quickly discover if it's awkward to bring up your topic, how clunky it is to go from category to category, where you've overwritten, and when it sounds artificial. Words may look great on paper or a computer screen, but as soon as you say them, their flaws become apparent.

Here are four guidelines to assist you in rewriting your routine.

Introduce the Routine

It's so unnatural to just come on stage and start saying your first joke. You'll want to bring up the subject matter of your routine in the same way that you'd bring it up in normal conversation. You can do this in one of three ways.

State the Topic

The purpose is to bring up your subject matter in a conversational manner, so when I say "state," I don't mean you should simply say, "I'd like to talk about the post office." Actually, that's not a bad approach, but if you have a show with several routines it'll soon become repetitive. There are as many ways of bringing up your topic as there are topics, but please don't ask the cliché question, "How many people here . . . ?" Be original.

Proclaim the Punch–Premise

Sometimes stating the topic isn't enough because the routine requires more information for it to make sense. When this is the case, proclaiming your punch–premise, including its negative opinion, will add the needed information to frame the routine. Just copying the punch–premise from the Joke Map probably won't suffice; you'll have to write it as a regular thought. The rules for creating a punch–premise in the Joke Map are for the purpose of writing jokes, not performing them.

PRESENT THE SETUP–PREMISE

Some routines will have more of an impact by presenting the setup–premise's positive opinion, which will often be performed as sarcasm. In such instances, word your setup–premise conversationally, rather than transcribing it directly from the Joke Map.

Deciding whether you introduce your routine with the topic, the punch–premise, or the setup–premise is best settled by trying them all. It'll often be a matter of which one lends itself to the best misdirection or which one doesn't give away the joke. Figuring this out will become easier with experience.

Add Segues

Segues are transitions between categories. (They're also used between routines or jokes, but not here.) Personally, I find most segues to be a waste of time. They're old-fashioned and harbor many of the comics' clichés I loathe so much. I believe the best segue is when the comedian just stops to think; the audience will know that a new topic, punch–premise, setup–premise, or category is about to follow. When a routine is just too clumsy without a few segues, by all means write them in, but do so sparingly.

Reword It Conversationally

This is where saying your jokes out loud is especially important. The idea is to phrase a joke just as you would say it in a social situation. I have my students improvise a bit before they get into their show. Then, if their behavior or language patterns change, everyone in the class can observe it. Basically, you're going to have to model what you do naturally so you can repeat it just as naturally in unnatural circumstances.

Search for a Story Line

At this point, what you have are clusters of jokes in categories. As you read the jokes out loud and play with the order, notice if there's a pattern within all this material to support a small story line. When I say story line, I don't mean a plot for a play or a movie, but rather a mini–story that will help you move logically though your categories. It can be as simple as going somewhere or doing something.

For instance, as I read the post office jokes out loud, I noticed a story about me going to the post office, waiting in line, trashing the post office, verbal bantering with a postal worker, then asking him questions about stamps. No Academy Award-winning plot, but it does show a progression of actions and motivations linking my jokes together into a coherent routine.

Based on all this advice, I'm going to rewrite the routine and explain some of the changes I've made. The additions and changes are underlined, but you'll have to figure out for yourself what's been edited out.

To start, I need to introduce the *service* jokes. Since I don't think the punch–premise or the setup–premise are necessary for the routine to make sense, I'm simply going to state the topic. To do this effectively I need to find the phrasing which expresses my feeling about the post office. How about this:

> How can I bring up the subject of the post office without sounding angry? I can't. So, here we go. First of all, the post office has a logo of an eagle streaking through the sky. Yeah, right. It should be something more like a slug taking a nap. It frustrates me because the post office is a monopoly. If it had to operate like a real business, it'd be about as successful as a steak house in India. Just the term *postal service* is an oxymoron.

Notice that I introduced the topic by being too angry to try to be clever—which I think was rather clever—and I added some words that make the sentences flow when they're spoken aloud.

Now, I have to add the *lines* jokes to the *service* jokes. However, the last *service* joke about oxymoron doesn't really fit with the first joke in the *lines* category about the Matterhorn. So, I'm editing the Matterhorn joke out. That doesn't mean I'm throwing it away; I'll put it into the *miscellaneous* category in case I find a place for it later. All I have left is the joke about closing the window, but it needs a little buffer at the beginning as a transition to the next thought:

> To show you what I mean, I was standing in a really long line for about ten minutes and it's getting even longer, so I yelled, "The line is getting longer. Can you please close one of the windows?" They did.

I'm not very happy with this because it makes a long joke even longer, but I think the joke is funny so I'll put up with it for now. I also added the word, *please* because I thought it helped to establish the target assumption, "open another window."

Next I'll splice the *postal workers* category onto the end of the *lines* joke. As I've mentioned before, the first joke about guns is phrased too much like a joke, so I'll attempt to word it more conversationally.

> Maybe I'm being too tough on postal workers. After all, they are actually very efficient—with guns. Hey, their motto is "Neither snow, nor rain, nor gloom of night shall keep them from their rounds." And the thing that gets me, I don't understand why so many postal workers get killed by other postal workers. You'd think they'd be killed by disgruntled customers.

As I evaluate the rest of this category, I find that the joke about the mug shot just doesn't fit. So I'll edit it out and put it in the *miscellaneous* category. The remainder of the category will go like this:

> After hearing me trash the post office, a postal worker said to me, "You shouldn't insult postal workers." I said, "Why not?" He said, "Because we know where you live." I said, "Even if you did come after me, you'd just show up at the wrong house."

That's better. This category works more effectively as a whole without the employee of the month joke. I really like that joke, though, so I'm sure I'll be able to squeeze it in later.

Finally, there's a bit of a jump from the *postal workers* category to the *stamps* category. This is one of those instances where a segue is appropriate. But, I'm still going to make it logical, short, and devoid of all comics' clichés. Sometimes, stating a version of the punch–premise or setup–premise will suffice as the segue, but here I've provided a link by continuing to converse with the postal worker.

> To change the subject a little bit, I asked him, "Why is it that the people who design stamps have never done one honoring the post office?" He said, "I think they're afraid people will spit on the wrong side."

These next few jokes don't stand on their own, so I'll have to state a conversational version of my punch–premise:

Here's something that bothers me, why is it that the post office has stamps of famous people like Marilyn Monroe, Martin Luther King—what I want to know is where's the commemorative series celebrating Charles Manson? And another thing, stamps only depict old-fashioned inventions, like the steam engine or the cotton gin. What about the important modern inventions, like the breast implant? Hey, I'd become a collector. They could release them in pairs. Of course, guys would lick them on both sides.

The leftovers are in the *miscellaneous* category:

I don't mind long lines if at the end I get to ride the Matterhorn.

I was checking out one of those mug shots of this particularly tough, nasty looking, lowlife—it was the employee of the month.

Many of the introductions, segues, and little conversational snippets were rewritten several times before I found a version I liked. They say Neil Simon rewrites his plays somewhere between twenty and thirty times. Assembling a routine may require hours of going over and over the same material until it feels right to you.

I'm not finished rewriting yet. First, I want to string my gems all together to see if I have a routine with a intelligible story line. Doing this, I'll read the routine out loud again and see if anything needs reordering, editing, tagging, or if I can find a place for the miscellaneous jokes. Any changes I'll mark with a double underline.

How can I bring up the subject of the post office without sounding angry. I can't. So, here we go. First of all, the post office has the audacity to have the logo of an eagle streaking through the sky. Yeah, right. It should be something more like a slug taking a nap. It frustrates me because the post office is a monopoly. If it had to operate like a real business, it'd be about as successful as a steak house in India. Just the term *postal service* is an oxymoron. The other day, I was standing in line and I was checking out one of those mug shots of this particularly tough, nasty looking, lowlife— it was the employee of the month. I'd been in line for about ten minutes and it's getting even longer, so I yelled, "The line is getting longer, can you please close one of the windows." They did. Maybe I'm being too tough on postal workers, after all, they are actually very efficient—with guns. Hey, their motto is: "Neither snow, nor rain, nor gloom of night shall keep them from their *rounds.*" And the thing that gets me, I don't understand why so many postal workers kill other postal workers. You'd think they'd be killed by disgruntled customers. After hearing me trash the post office, a postal worker said to me, "You shouldn't insult postal workers." I said, "Why not?" He said, "Because we know where you live." I said, "Even if you did come after me, you'd show up at the wrong house." To change the subject a little bit, I asked him, "Why is it that the artists who design stamps have never done one honoring the post office?" He said, "I think they're afraid people will spit on the wrong side." Here's something else that bothers me, why is it that the post office has stamps of famous people like Marilyn Monroe, Martin Luther King—what I want to know is where's the commemorative series celebrating Charles Manson? And another thing, stamps only depict old-fashioned inventions, like the cotton gin or the steam engine. What about the important modern inventions, like the breast implant? They could release them in pairs. Hey, I'd be a collector. Of course, guys would lick them on both sides.

Miscellaneous

I don't mind long lines if at the end I get to ride the Matterhorn.

There it is—the best I can do on paper or computer screen. Notice that I got the "employee of the month" joke in as well as a segue which placed me in the post office line. That made the reference to standing in line in the "close the window" joke redundant, so I took it out. I also left out the Matterhorn joke, which I never really liked anyway. And I switched the order of the invention joke tags 1 and 2 because it just felt better when I said it out loud.

There's still one more problem: It bothers me that the routine has two jokes about saliva—the "tribute to the post office" joke, which has the phrase "spit on the wrong side," and the breast implant joke that says, "lick both sides." I like them both, so I'll perform them first to see which is the stronger before making a decision about which one to keep.

Of course, this is just a first draft. It isn't finished now, and never will be. It will change as I rehearse it, perform it, then rewrite it again, and again, and again. Assembling a routine isn't a destination, it's a journey.

6

Points of View
Narrator, Self, Character

Watching a comic shift from one point of view (POV) to another within a story or by acting them out has always been an integral aspect of stand-up comedy. Yet, this fundamental technique has never been formally analyzed and discussed to clearly lay out its vast array of applications. As you begin to understand the uses of POVs, you'll discover how important a tool they are for putting together a show and making people laugh.

This chapter begins by defining the three basic POVs. It ends with an exercise designed to teach you how to stage shifting POVs for stand-up comedy.

Narrator POV: how you perceive things as a nonparticipant or observer
Self POV: how you perceive things as a participant
Character POV: how you perceive things as someone or something else

Let's take these one at a time and look at an example of each.

Narrator POV: How You Perceive Things as a Nonparticipant or Observer

In Narrator POV, the comedian is never directly involved in the experience the joke is about, but observes, reports, talks about, or . . . narrates it. This is a very common approach in the joke-telling style of stand-up. For instance, the following joke is stated entirely from Narrator POV:

> Last night, I was talking to my friend Bob when I mentioned that I was recently sitting at a stop sign and this car rear-ended me. He asked if I was hurt. I told him that I couldn't tell until I talked to my lawyer.

As long as the comedian relates to the experience within the joke as something being talked about rather than something being reenacted, it's from a Narrator POV.

Self POV: How You Perceive Things as a Participant

When doing Self POV, the comedian is involved in the experience, which is acted out as if it's happening in the present. Since audiences want to hang out with the comedian, it's much more fun being involved in the scenario that is happening rather than one just being described. Here's the same joke with both Narrator and Self POVs.

Narrator: Last night, I was talking to my friend Bob when I mentioned,
Self: "I was sitting at a stop sign and this guy rear-ended me."
Narrator: Bob asked if I was hurt. I told him,
Self: "I can't tell until I talk to my lawyer."

The difference between Narrator POV and Self POV can be confusing because they are both *you*. But remember, when you're in Narrator POV you're explaining, setting up, making an observation, or talking about something you're not currently participating in; when you're in Self POV you're participating or reenacting an experience as if it's happening.

Character POV: How You Perceive Things as Someone or Something Else

Character POV is anyone or anything the comedian can act out as a character. This includes people, impersonations, animals, objects, and concepts such as emotions. Here's a variation of same joke including the Character POV:

Narrator: Last night, I was talking to my friend Bob when I mentioned,
Self: "I was sitting at a stop sign and this guy rear-ended me."
Character: "Were you hurt?"
Self: "I can't tell until I talk to my lawyer."

For my taste, this is a much more interesting joke to perform because there's a conversation happening that the audience becomes involved in.

In my classes, I've had students populate the stage with a whole slew of Character POVs by recreating family reunions, business meetings, parties—one student actually did the different personalities in his head. It takes a bit of acting ability and know-how to keep the different characters clear and distinct so the audience can follow such a complex scene. But it's worth it because it makes for such interesting stand-up comedy.

POV Exercise

How a comedian uses POVs is a matter of style. Everyone uses them whether they're aware of it or not. Observation comedians operate exclusively from Narrator POV; character oriented comedians submerge themselves in a vast array of Character POVs. Most comics employ some form of all three of the basic POVs. How you incorporate them is up to you.

To help you learn how the three basic POVs apply to stand-up comedy, I've devised an exercise that uses an argument and is done in four rounds. As you go through this exercise, it will be helpful to take notes. Use a separate piece of paper along with the POV Exercise Form (page 87). In Round 1 you explore the argument from the Self POV only. In Round 2 you take on the other side of the argument, doing only the Character POV. In Round 3 you shift back and forth between Self POV and Character POV. In Round 4 you employ all three POVs, starting with the Narrator POV to set the scene, then portraying the argument by shifting between Self POV and Character POV, and occasionally popping back to Narrator POV to make some intermittent remarks.

Here are some guidelines for the type of argument that is effective for this exercise. (Note that these rather restrictive guidelines apply to this exercise only.)

- It must be an argument between you, Self POV, and some other adult human Character POV. (No animals, children, cartoons, etc.).
- The other adult (Character POV) must be a person you can por-

tray. Since in Round 2 you'll only be enacting Character POV, you must be able to become that person and act out his or her side of the argument.

- The argument must be done standing up and face to face (no phone).
- The argument must have multiple issues so it will sustain itself for three or four minutes.

This exercise works much better if it's based on a real argument, although it doesn't have to be one you've actually been involved in. Don't try to recreate the argument exactly—just use it as a starting point so you can have fun and let it become whatever you want. This is an opportunity to say all of those things you probably didn't say in the original argument.

Avoid choosing an argument that's so fresh or heart-wrenching it'll put you through changes. This is an exercise to help you learn a stand-up technique, not psychocomedy.

Following the guidelines above, select an argument. If you don't understand the roles of Narrator POV, Self POV, and Character POV, go back over the preceding section until you do. Assuming that you do understand and that you've chosen an argument, you're ready to do the exercise.

Round 1: Self POV Only

In Round 1 you become Self POV *only* to carry on the argument you've chosen with an imagined Character POV. Here is how it's staged. Self POV stands facing the imagined Character POV as in any conversation. It's also imperative that you identify where your audience is located because ultimately you'll be performing POVs for them which will effect your staging.

To help establish some basic information about the scene, ask and answer the following questions:

Where is the Character POV standing?

Who are you arguing with?

What is the Character POV wearing?

Where does this argument take place?

What are you arguing about?

One more thing: Remember to *listen* to what the imaginary Character POV has to say. Whenever you make some point, stop talking so the Character POV has time to make a rebuttal. It'll amaze you how this will change the direction of the argument.

Once you've answered these questions and you're ready to assume Self POV while imagining the Character POV, *begin Round 1*. If after about three or four minutes the argument comes to a natural climax, end it. If the argument ends after a minute or less, you'll need to choose an argument with more issues so it can go on for several minutes and begin again.

When finished, think about what you've learned and write down any important revelations, then continue on to Round 2.

Round 2: Character POV Only

In Round 2 you'll be portraying the Character POV *only*. This means you become the person who is your Character POV and take on his or her side of the argument. To do this, you must *physically change sides* by stepping into the spot where the Character POV was previously visualized standing.

Here is the challenge for Round 2: You must totally give up the position you expressed as Self POV and take on the other side of the argument. To do this effectively, you must understand how the Character POV is *right from his or her perspective*.

Before beginning Round 2, it's helpful if you establish the personality of the Character POV. Once you have a handle on how to act like this person, you'll find it easier to get into the argument. Following are two acting tips.

CHOOSE A VOICE DIFFERENT FROM YOUR OWN THAT'S RIGHT FOR THE CHARACTER

Having a particular voice you can focus on helps settle you into a character. If you're a guy and your Character POV is a woman you might raise your voice to falsetto range. Conversely, if you're a woman portraying a man, lower your voice a tad. Also, if the character has a particular vocal idiosyncrasy, do your best to mimic it; it doesn't have to be exact. This exercise isn't about doing an impersonation of the person you're portraying. You're only changing your voice to get the gist of the person. And make sure to choose a voice you can sustain for a several-minute argument.

TAKE ON A POSTURE DIFFERENT FROM YOUR OWN THAT'S RIGHT FOR THE CHARACTER

A distinct posture, mannerism, or physical idiosyncracy really helps you find a character quickly. If a man is portraying a woman he might adopt effeminate body language; and if a woman is acting as if she is a man maintain a masculine posture.

Play with the voice and posture of the Character POV until you feel relatively comfortable with it. If you can't seem to get into it, then pick another argument with a Character POV you feel you can portray and start all over again. Just as with Round 1, you must *listen* to the other side of the argument, which is in this case—your own. Again, it'll fuel the conflict.

Once all of this is established, *begin Round 2*, acting out the Character POV side of the argument. The argument should last three or four minutes, the same as in Round 1. Again, if it lasts less than a minute, go back to Round 1 and start over.

When you're finished, write down anything you want to remember, and continue on to Round 3.

Round 3: Self POV and Character POV

In Round 3 you play both Self POV and Character POV, shifting back and forth between the two sides. You'll want to practice shifting a few times before getting into the argument. One of the most common mistakes beginning students make is *mixing up the sides* the POVs are on. It's confusing when the audience accepts a Self POV on the left side and a Character POV on the right side, and then switch sides for no apparent reason, or, even worse, both stand on the same side facing the same direction. If you're uncertain which side each POV is on, the confusion will be reflected in your performance. It's so important to consistently establish the Self POV on one side and the Character POV on the other. If you're absolutely clear in your rehearsal where each POV is, then your performance will be easy to follow.

When you decide to shift from Self POV to Character POV, take *one step* to the other side and find the Character POVs voice and posture. There is one main rule for shifting between Self POV and Character POV: The Performer must remain facing the audience. Not turning your back to the audience is a matter of good staging. Try shifting back and forth several times until it's effortless to go from Self POV to the new voice and posture of Character POV and back again. As you get better at this, you'll only need to pivot your weight from one heel to the other to face the opposite direction. A more advanced technique is just turning your face back and forth.

This is usually where the humor really starts coming into the scene. The two POVs may start saying nasty, sarcastic, mean, insulting, and other fun things to each other. If the argument takes on a life of its own, let it. But remember, this isn't psychodrama; it's an exercise in comedy technique. Allow the jokes to flow.

Once you're comfortable shifting from Self POV to Character POV, *start Round 3.*

If the argument has a natural climax and ending, then let it run its course. If not, end it at the height of the argument; about four or five minutes should be enough.

When finished, sit down and think about what you've learned from doing the exercise. Focus on whether or not you shifted easily into the Character POV and if you remained facing the audience when shifting. If you discovered any good jokes or bits write them down. When you're finished, do Round 4.

Round 4: Self POV, Character POV, and Narrator POV

In Round 4, you're doing all three POVs. You've already rehearsed Self POV and Character POV; now it's time to add Narrator POV which is *the only position that talks directly to the audience.* This serves two very important functions. First, Narrator POV sets up the scene by explaining *who* Character POV is, *what* the argument is about, and *where* this takes place. Second, he occasionally reappears to move the scene along and/or to make smart-aleck chides about what's happening in the scene. Please, avoid using Narrator POV as a Freudian analysis of the scene—this isn't Psychology 101; it's Comedy Technique 101.

For the staging, it's important to remember the audience is located in front of you. Narrator POV stands back and outside the argument with the Self POV and Character POV between the Narrator POV and the imagined audience. Once Narrator POV has set up the scene, you can step forward into Self POV or Character POV to get into the argument just as you did in Round 3. After five to eight shifts of the argument, pop back out of the argument into Narrator POV by simply stepping back or away from the audience. This keeps the visualized images of Self POV and Character POV between you and the audience so you can refer to them when making comments. Then step from Narrator POV forward into Self POV or Character POV to continue the argument. Again, after five to eight shifts into the argument between Self POV and Character POV, pop out of the scene to Narrator POV and make a brief smart-aleck remark based on what's happening in the scene.

For example, one of my students, a sweet, petite blonde who always wore a bow in her hair told me that she didn't understand what I meant by making comments based on the scene. So I asked her to show me her argument. She demurely explained from Narrator POV, "Well, it's between me and my boyfriend." To my surprise, in her argument this timid princess became a raging tyrant.

Self POV: You bastard, I'll kick you in the nuts so hard they'll come out your nose.
Character POV: I'm going to rip off your head and shit down your neck.
Self POV: Lorena Bobbitt didn't go far enough for me; you'll wake up some morning and I'll be juggling your cock and balls.

At this point, I said "Pop out," and she did. I stood next to her and said, "Look at these two arguing. What do you want to say about them?" She laced her fingers together and sighed, "They're in love." The class laughed for about two minutes. Of course, your remarks don't need to be this extreme. You'll do fine with jibes like, "Does anyone have any boxing gloves?" or "Oh great, I've officially become my father." Get the idea?

Begin Round 4, including five or six pop-outs to Narrator POV, for six to eight minutes and then end it, or allow the argument to come to its natural conclusion.

You have gone through four rounds of building an argument with three POVs. Because you experienced the argument from the Character POV and Narrator POV as well as the original Self POV, your memory of it will be more detailed than the actual event. The argument will be more like a holographic memory.

Now, sit down and reflect on the entire process. Write down the differences you noticed by experiencing the argument from three different POVs. If you developed a funny bit through doing the exercise, consider using it as the basis for a routine. If it wasn't particularly funny, do it all over again using the form on page 87. And this time pick an argument you can have more fun with.

Streamlining the POV Exercise

Initially I teach this exercise in four rounds so you can clearly define the three roles and understand how to keep them separate, but you can condense the whole process from four rounds to one. By doing Round 4 only, you can streamline the exercise by starting with Narrator POV to set the scene. Then play it out by shifting back and forth between Self POV and Character POV, occasionally popping out to Narrator POV to make some snide remarks or add exposition.

You don't always have to do an argument, but I find this exercise works best with situations that evoke extreme emotions. Try scenes that involve suspicion, disgust, guilt, etc. Without an extreme emotional through line, the scene may get boring rather quickly because the Self POV and Character POV will have no passionate drive to converse.

If you don't understand the three basic POVs and their staging well enough to streamline the four rounds into one, go through the original four-round process again until you do.

POV Applications

POVs are a robust technique with a wide range of uses with implication throughout my entire comedy technique. The more you explore and play with POVs, the more applications you'll find to help you express your personal style of being funny. Following are a few of those applications:

Joke Structure

As you learned earlier, all jokes are essentially *two interpretations of one thing*: the target assumption being the expected interpretation and the reinterpretation being the surprising interpretation. Once you truly understand the implications of this model you'll quickly realize there are a multitude of ways this can be accomplished, including shifting from one POV to another. That is to say, shifting from Narrator POV

POV Exercise Form

Select an Argument:
- Between you and an adult human.
- The other adult must be a person you can portray.
- Argument done standing up and face to face (no phone).
- Have multiple issues.

Notes:

Round 1: Self POV Only
- Who are you arguing with?
- Where does this argument take place?
- What are you arguing about?
- Three or four minutes.
- Begin.

Notes:

Round 2: Character POV Only
- Choose a different voice and posture.
- Stand on the opposite side.
- Make the Character POV *right* from his or her perspective.
- Three or four minutes.
- Begin.

Notes:

Round 3: Self POV and Character POV
- Shift *one* step between POVs.
- For Character POV change your voice and posture.
- Allow the jokes to flow.
- Four or five minutes.
- Begin.

Notes:

Round 4: Self POV, Character POV, and Narrator POV
- Self POV and Character POV are staged between Narrator POV and audience.
- Narrator talks to the audience and sets the scene.
- Argue by shifting between Self and Character POV
- Five or six times pop out to Narrator POV and make remarks.
- Six to eight minutes.
- Begin.

Final notes:

to Self POV or Self POV to Character POV or Character POV to Narrator POV all constitute joke structure because they contain two interpretations from two different perspectives.

Here's a joke I tell about visiting San Francisco:

> I was standing on a street corner when a bum came up to me and demanded, "Hey Buddy. Give me *five* dollars." I turned to him and said, "When did you get a raise?"

I chose to introduce this with the traditional Narrator POV: "I was standing on a street corner when a bum came up to me and demanded," then I shifted into Character POV became the bum and demanded, "Hey Buddy. Give me *five* dollars." As I stepped from Character POV to Self POV, I made the quick Narrator POV comment, "I turned to him and said," then settled into Self POV and retorted with the punch, "When did you get a raise?"

Notice how the shift in POV from Character to Self structures this joke. The connector is the bum's action of *demanding five dollars*. The target assumption is that *the bum is demanding five dollars because he doesn't have a job*. The reinterpretation is that *the bum is demanding five dollars because that is his job*. The two interpretations of *demanding five dollars* that came from two separate POVs is what structures this joke.

Shifting between the three POVs offers the possibility of joke structure not just because it allows you to interpret one thing in two ways, but also in three.

Generating Material

Every joke is loaded with associations about relationships and environments. I often refer to this associated information as the "experience." Since shifting POVs is a mechanism for structuring jokes, whenever you physically position yourself to become another person, an animal, or an object, or you pretend that you're in a particular environment, the information in that experience becomes fodder for jokes.

When you explore the psychology of your Self POV or a Character POV, you'll be surprised at the depth of the experience. For instance, a student, Dave Reinitz, was doing a bit about getting his car towed away. The story line took him to the impound yard where he was confronted by the guy he must pay to get his car back. The first time Dave did this exchange with the Impound Guy, he only did a greeting, then rushed on to several jokes about his car. I suggested that he explore the Character POV of the Impound Guy and allow him to talk.

David took the time to act out the Impound Guy, explore his view of the world, and discover what he had to say. The following week he came into class with this bit in which the Impound Guy is a raspy-voiced, pint-of-hooch-under-the-counter smart-ass:

Dave: Hi. I'm here to pick up my car.
Impound Guy: No shit. And I thought you were here to visit the supermodels in the back. Or perhaps you'd like a tour of our botanical gardens. It's enchanting this time of year, what with the dandelion and stink weed in bloom. Now which friggin' car is yours?
Dave: The blue Ferrari.
Impound Guy: "Hah. You're here for the Pinto wagon, aren't ya? (*to his helper, Lou, in the back*) Hey, Lou, bring up the Pinto wagon with the Mondale bumper sticker. And Lou, you owe me ten bucks—he showed up for it. Do you want to go double or nothing on the pink Gremlin?

These are not the kinds of jokes you'd normally write with a pen and paper or computer. They come from imagining how you or a character would behave in a given situation. And the best way to do this is by becoming the character and exploring the circumstances by improvising.

Bringing the Material into the Present

Material has a far greater impact on an audience when it's reenacted as if it's happening in the present. I was first introduced to this phenomenon by numerous books on acting which mention that even if a section of dialogue is stated in past tense, the actor must behave as if it's happening in the present. Several of my acting coaches reiterated this idea.

Now, let's relate this to applying POVs. Since Narrator POV is a nonparticipating observer, all material is presented in past, future, or fantasy tense. This isn't bad; in fact, it's necessary for setting up some jokes and routines. But when the entire routine or show remains in Narrator POV, the experiences are *never* related to as if they're happening in the present.

On the other hand, when you move your material into Self POV and Character POV, which are participants in the experience being reenacted, these experiences happen before the audience's very eyes.

An example of bringing material into the present was demonstrated by my student Danny Walsh, who came into class with this joke:

> Last night my wife came out of the bedroom and asked me if her new dress made her look fat. I told her, no, it was all that blubber hanging from her ass that made her look fat.

This is a good joke, but it was all phrased from Narrator POV. I suggested to Danny that it would be much stronger if he brought it into the present by portraying his Self POV and her Character POV. In class that following week, Danny did this:

Narrator: My wife came out of the bedroom last night and did one of these. . . .
Wife: (*girlishly twirls around*) Does this new dress make me look fat?
Narrator: I said,
Self: No, honey. What makes you look fat is all that blubber hanging from your ass.

This was essentially the same joke told to the same audience of students, yet it got a bigger laugh. It's funnier because the wife is actually there to hear Danny's cruel punch, and Danny is actually saying it to her. This is a wonderful lesson on the power of bringing material into the present.

Identifying and Portraying the Character (POV)s

Once you begin to identify all the Character POVs in your material, you'll be astounded at how plentiful they are. The basic method for doing this is to never tell the audience what someone or something says or does. Instead, become that someone or something and let them say or do it. Portraying Character POVs is one of the most overlooked techniques in comedy. Yet, those who do a lot of characters in their shows know just how effective they are at getting laughs.

A student, Matthew Arzt, was doing a bit on how disgusting the talk shows have become. One joke was about giving a talk show to Arnold Schwartzenegger. It was a funny idea, but I thought it could be even funnier if Matthew actually became Arnold as the talk show host. The next week, Matthew surprised everyone by nailing Arnold's Austrian accent in this bit:

Narrator POV: I hear they're considering giving a talk show to Arnold. I can imagine what that's going to look like.
As Arnold: We're here—to cut you down. Today on Arnold, "Dress like a tramp or I'm leaving you."

Of course, Character POVs aren't always people; they can also be animals. Most people already tend to project their own thoughts and feelings onto animals. This is only one step away from portraying the animals in a show.

A student, John Willey, used the concept of how people and animals perceive time differently to create this piece about his cat:

> If one year to a human is seven years to a cat, then for the cat one day equals a week. So along about six o'clock I'm sure my cat starts thinking, "He's never coming back. He probably ran into the street. I'm gonna have to learn to use the can opener. But first, I'll have to develop an opposable thumb."

Character POVs can also be objects like cars, toilets, or parts of our bodies. They can even be abstractions such as emotions or the concept of dysfunction—almost anything can be personified into a character. Character POVs are only limited by your imagination.

Richard Pryor is, in my opinion, the master of unusual POVs. If you want a great lesson on how to utilize POVs, especially Character POVs, rent any one of Pryor's concert videos and enjoy the variety and originality of his portrayals. There's the heart attack sequence when his heart speaks to him; the trip to Africa bit where the stink from one of the natives engulfs him; and my favorite, his portrayal of his cocaine pipe—one of the most brilliant, insightful, and tragic comedy routines ever recorded.

Expressing Your Opinions

If you're willing to be vulnerable enough to put your honest thoughts and feelings into your show, you'll be surprised at how many people will identify with you. This is, to me, what Lenny Bruce brought to comedy. Most people remember him for his foul language and the court cases that followed. But it was his willingness to say exactly what was on his mind, in joke form, that created a whole new style of stand-up comedy and altered the perception of how to come up with material. Before Bruce, the approach was to either come up with any kind of joke that would get a laugh or develop a comical character. Lenny Bruce found his comic voice in his own head, not in a joke that would please other people. Fortunately or unfortunately, what was on his mind was sex and drugs, along with some relevant social issues. Bruce's ability to brazenly pontificate on his personal views opened a portal to an infinite comedic universe for the next generation of comics—the likes of George Carlin, Richard Pryor, Elaine Boosler, Bill Hicks, Sam Kinison, and many more.

When you choose an experience and improvise on it from Self POV and Narrator POV, you'll be shocked to discover how opinionated you are. Acting out an experience as if it's happening is a wonderful opportunity for honesty because there are no consequences. In comedy, you can say all those things you've been thinking, but were afraid to let out. For instance, here's Carrie Snow's view of men:

> I always wanted a boyfriend in prison cause I'd always know where he was.

Using Character POVs allows you to say or do things in front of an audience that you'd never do in public. If the audience finds it offensive, you can always blame it on the Character POV. With the right approach, comics can say almost anything without consequence to themselves.

When I was the opening act for the male strippers at Chippendale's, I wrote a joke that I thought was very funny but I would never do as myself—especially in front of an all-female crowd. The joke went:

> Sure women want equal rights—but are they willing to fuck for them?

A funny joke, but the audience would hate me for saying it. Being an artist, my devious mind found a solution. I'd give it to a character who could and would say it without realizing how offensive it really is. Enter the Character POV—Bob Hormone. He's the kind of jerk who leaves the three top buttons of his shirt undone, calls women "babe," and points his index finger as if it's the barrel of a pistol as a greeting. When Bob said the joke, it was as much a comment on the kind of idiots who actually think this way as it was as a lampooning of the women's movement. Both sides take a shot. The joke worked great.

When you use POVs to put yourself into an experience and improvise, you'll often find those opinions that everyone else spends their life trying to hide from others. Your job as a comedian is to boldly express those opinions, but remember to do it in joke structure.

Combining (POV)s

The fundamental concept of POVs is really quite simple, yet there are so many variations that can be woven into a complex performance. There'll be times when you'll want to do a joke as Self POV being in a situation, such as driving a car through a desert, then sarcastically comment from Narrator POV about how you remember when this area was nothing but over crowded strip malls. Also you may want to joke about a Character POV doing one thing, such as stealing merchandise, all the while explaining with your voice as Narrator POV that the character is really just an entrepreneur. Yet another variation is having a Character POV become another Character POV as with this joke by my student Mel McKee.

Narrator POV: As a high school teacher I've had students begin doing "your mama" jokes. In class, one kid yelled at me,
Character POV: "Your mama's so fat that when she takes a bath the *water* gets out and says,
Character POV: 'I'll wait.'"

The Character POV of the student acts out another Character POV of the water. Since I can't possibly go over all of the combinations, you'll have to discover them on your own through experimentation. Keep in mind that POVs are an easy means of constructing jokes because each shift constitutes joke structure. Play with them freely.

Foundation for Rehearsing

As you'll discover in the next chapter, POVs are the cornerstone of my Rehearsal Process. To foreshadow a bit, you're usually considered funniest when you're talking about things that have really happened to you. So when you rehearse a joke as an experience, you'll not only be reenacting Self POV, but also Narrator POV and relevant Character POVs. This method of rehearsal creates a holographic memory of the whole experience, which is far superior to simply memorizing the words of a joke.

When it comes to style, there's no right or wrong because POVs are flexible enough to fit anyone's style. The more you play with them, the more you'll understand how they apply to clear staging, generating material, bringing material into the present, identifying and portraying characters, expressing your opinions, rehearsing, and performing. A knowledge of POVs opens the door to comic possibilities that are virtually limitless. And beyond that, portraying POVs is just plain fun.

7

Rehearsing

Most people believe that all they have to do to be a comedian is memorize a bunch of jokes, then get on stage and tell them. But it's not that simple. Have you ever told a joke that got a huge laugh in one situation and a roar of silence in another? That's precisely why doing stand-up comedy involves much more than just telling jokes.

SECRET #8:
COMEDIANS INTERPRET JOKES IN WAYS THAT MAKE PEOPLE LAUGH.

What makes a joke funny? The comic's ability to read a situation and use the information to interpret the joke in a way that will make that particular audience laugh. Consistently making people laugh is an act of creativity; it takes a great deal of experience. As much as my analytical techniques may do to demystify the structure of comedy, the talent to make people laugh remains a magical phenomenon.

As a teacher, I find students have many more performing problems that need to be solved than writing problems. Joke writing problems can usually be eliminated with practice, time, and effort, but performing problems will keep a student stuck at the same level until they're solved. I've found that *almost all performing problems are a result of improper rehearsal.*

Have you ever been really funny around friends or family, at work or at a party, and thought, "If I could only do this on stage, I'd be a great stand-up comedian?" Well, you're right. The ingredients that go into being really funny in informal surroundings are the same ones that make for an excellent stand-up comedy performance.

Let's examine what goes on when you're being really funny. (When I talk about "being funny," I mean acting spontaneously, not sitting around telling old jokes.) You're telling a story about something that actually happened to you, reliving it as if it's happening again, freely expressing or exaggerating the same emotions you had at the time, becoming the other people, maybe even animals and objects, stopping to let your listeners laugh, speeding up or slowing down according to their response, not criticizing yourself—probably because of the effects of drugs or alcohol—and, most importantly, having a great deal of fun. Does that pretty much cover it?

To express your real sense of humor on a stand-up comedy stage, you have to be funny in the same way that you've been funny all your life. The rehearsal techniques you'll learn in this chapter will help you replicate this natural manner of being funny whenever you want. In my experience I've found improper rehearsal to be the number one factor that causes people to lose touch with their natural sense of humor.

SECRET #9:

HOW YOU REHEARSE IS HOW YOU WILL PERFORM.

If you rehearse by pacing back and forth, looking at the ground and trying to remember what you're supposed to say next, then you'll perform pacing back and forth, staring at the ground, and still trying to remember what you're supposed to say next. Conversely, if you rehearse a joke as if it were something that really happened to you, pretending that you're relating to an audience and having fun with your material, then you'll perform as if the material really happened to you, you'll relate to the audience, and you'll have fun.

Rehearsing material in a different manner than you want to perform it is an error I often refer to as the "Milkman Syndrome." This name was inspired by a student in my advanced class who had a good sense of humor but who would forget everything he'd rehearsed whenever he did his show. I asked him if he was rehearsing his show at home, and he assured me that he was. When I asked for more details about his rehearsal process, he informed me that he was a milkman and would rehearse while driving between stops. When I heard that it was immediately clear to me what the problem was. I asked the student to get back on stage, sit on the stool, put his feet on one of the tables, and pretend to drive his milk truck. Though a little embarrassed, he acquiesced to my bizarre request. To his and the entire class's amazement, as soon as he assumed the same body position he'd been in while rehearsing, he remembered his show perfectly.

The lesson here is that since the performance state mimics the rehearsal state, it's extremely important to use a rehearsal process that will bring forth your natural state of being funny.

The Creator and the Critic

The *Creator* and the *Critic* are two facets of your personality. Both are essential to being a professional funny person, but they must be in balance—the Creator coming up with ideas and the Critic technically crafting the show. If the two aspects conflict, they'll cause problems that you may not even be aware of.

The functions of the Creator are inventing and expressing. The Creator is intuitive, imaginative, emotional, playful, eager to explore, and unafraid of making mistakes. It's the child in you, who doesn't care whether something's right or wrong as long as it's fun. In stand-up comedy, the Creator explores ideas for jokes, discovers even more when rehearsing, and interprets the material in a way that makes people laugh.

The Critic is concerned with improving and crafting. This aspect of your personality is intellectual, reality-based, analytical, goal-oriented, and judgmental. Like a parent within you, the Critic insists things be done right and is very serious about it. It notices all mistakes and wants them corrected. When you're assembling a stand-up comedy show, it's the Critic that crafts your ideas into joke structure and organizes the jokes into a show.

When people try to be creative and critical at the same time, the Creator and the Critic conflict and the effectiveness of both is canceled out. This problem is a result of ineffective rehearsal practices.

For example, while practicing his material, a comic may allow the Critic to interject a constant stream of negative comments through internal self-talk. It usually goes like this:

Creator: This guy goes into a confessional. He says to the minister . . .
Critic: That was terrible, it's not a minister, it's a priest. What's wrong with you? You're so stupid. It's a priest. Now, try it again.
Creator: This guy grows . . .

Critic: Grows? What the hell are you doing? Take it from the top.
Creator: This guy goes into a confessional.
Critic: You didn't pay your bills today. You're going to get late charges added on to them. Why did you stop? You idiot. Do it again.

If you're creative and self-critical at the same time when you rehearse, *you're rehearsing the Critic into your show.* This is a very important concept. Remember, how you rehearse is how you will perform. So if you rehearse the Critic into your show, how can you expect to be free of it when you perform? You can't. The Critic will consume your attention on stage just as thoroughly as it does during rehearsal.

Then the real trouble begins. With all of your attention focused on evaluating rather than doing the show, you go blank and forget your material. The Critic condemns you for screwing up, so you focus even more of your attention on yourself. To make matters worse, (yes, they can get worse) you're not paying attention to the audience, so how can you gather the information you need to interpret the jokes in a way that will make them laugh? You can't. Even if you do remember your jokes, they probably won't get a laugh. Then of course, it's the Critic's royal duty to chastise you for having this problem, which it created.

Separating the Creator and the Critic

You must train your Creator and your Critic to work independently of each other. When you want to invent and express, be the Creator only. When you want to improve and craft, be the Critic only. It sounds simple enough, but believe me, it's easier said than done. Most of us have spent a lifetime constantly criticizing ourselves; we're not sure how it got started, and we don't know how to stop it. And ignoring your Critic doesn't work either because it just yells even louder, sometimes to the point of taking over your whole mind. No wonder some comics turn to alcohol and drugs to shut it up.

The Critic's intent is to help you improve, so you don't want to get rid of it entirely. At the same time, you don't want it interfering with the Creator's ability to freely invent and express. What you do want is for your Creator and Critic to do their jobs without encroaching on each other's territory. How do you accomplish that?

The Critic Spot and the Rehearsal Space

You must rehearse in two physically separate locations. One allotted to the Critic, referred to as the *Critic Spot*, and the other assigned to the Creator, called the *Rehearsal Space*.

I want to stress how important it is to rehearse in two physically separate locations. You've been conditioned by years of trying to be creative and critical at the same time, so your mind doesn't view these as two separate functions. But when you assign functions to their own physically separate locations, a marvelous thing happens—your mind marks them as different. And when you do this over a period of time, your mind finally comes to understand that the Creator and the Critic can be more effective by doing their jobs at different times.

To truly divide the Creator and Critic, you must be absolutely consistent about keeping them in their own locations. When you're being the Creator in your Rehearsal Space, never allow the Critic to interrupt. If the Critic does come in, stop and move into the Critic Spot to get its information. When you feel you can practice without the Critic looking over your shoulder, go back to your Rehearsal Space.

When you're finished practicing in your Rehearsal Space, walk across the room to your Critic Spot and encourage your Critic to spew forth all of its comments. Keep in mind that the positive intent of your Critic is to help you improve and craft, but it should only be allowed to speak when you're in your Critic Spot. You want its help, but only at the appropriate time.

As your mind becomes accustomed to this split, you'll discover how liberating it is to rehearse free from the confines of the Critic's negative judgments. You'll also notice that when you're in your Critic Spot, you'll enjoy giving yourself feedback because instead of having to interrupt, that part of you will be acknowledged and appreciated for its contribution.

Why Rehearse?

Aptly enough, the word *rehearse* is distantly related to the old Norwegian word *hervi*, a rake-like tool used for cultivating. And that's exactly what rehearsal is—a tool for cultivating your show. Being funny is an act of creativity, so your show should be regarded as a growing entity. Rehearsal lays the groundwork for a show to evolve.

SECRET #10:

A JOKE IS A RESPONSE TO SOME EXPERIENCE.

When we spontaneously make up jokes, we're responding to sensory information received in the present or experienced in the mind as a memory or fantasy. We can't think up jokes about nothing (unless the joke is about nothing, but then nothing becomes the something the joke is about). The creation of a joke begins with a piece of information that comes into the mind; it is then formed into joke structure and expressed. I refer to all of this sensory information that's happening in the present, recalled as a memory, or conjured up as a fantasy an *experience*.

If you want to express your natural sense of humor, you must first remember an experience before responding with a joke. Likewise, to remember your show, you must implant experiences in your mind so you can respond to them in the form of fantasies, memories, and things happening in the present.

This brings up a big question: How do you tell a joke by recalling an experience?

The Mind Remembers in Pictures, Sounds, and Feelings

Our minds receive information only through the senses—what we see, hear, feel, taste, and smell. Since we can't recall actual tastes and smells, what we remember are *pictures*, *sounds*, and *feelings*. These are our means of perceiving, storing, and retrieving information. We *perceive* by seeing, hearing, and feeling in the present. We *store* information in our minds (unconsciously) as pictures, sounds, and feelings. And we *retrieve* information by remembering pictures, sounds, and feelings.

For instance, if I asked you what you did this morning just after waking up, you'd say something like, "I turned off the alarm clock, got out of bed, and took a shower." How did you remember that? Not by memorized words describing what happened. You were seeing pictures of your actions, which included the sounds and feelings that accompanied them. These pictures, sounds, and feelings constitute the experience.

Sensory Experiences Activate Human Behavior

Although you're probably not aware of it, your behavior is generated by the pictures, sounds, and feelings that enter the mind in the present and are stored in the unconscious mind, or have been retrieved as memories. Say, for example, you see someone you're sexually attracted to; that experience comes into your mind through your senses at that moment. By association, the experience triggers a memory of someone with whom you had an exciting sexual encounter in the past, which, in turn, causes you to fantasize about jumping the bones of the person who attracted you. As a result of all these sensory experiences, you get turned on. If your response is strong enough, you might even try to meet the person, get rejected, and revert to a self-maintenance program. All of this behavior was activated by pictures, sounds, and feelings experienced in the present through the senses or in the form of memories or fantasies.

Words Do *Not* Activate Human Behaviors

Our minds have been processing pictures, sounds, and feelings for millions of years, but language is a relatively recent development. The human mind wasn't designed to memorize words.

Words are symbols that represent experiences. Since they're just representations, they don't affect us as actual experiences do. Words are like a menu, whereas experiences are like a meal. Rehearsing jokes by memorizing the words is like going to a restaurant and eating the menu—it resembles the real thing, but it's not the real thing.

Take the word *funny*, for instance. Say it, write it, or think of it—you won't laugh. But if it causes you to remember the pictures, sounds, and feeling of a hilarious experience, you *will* laugh. And what makes you laugh will be the funny *experience*, not the word *funny*.

Memorizing the *Words* Is the *Worst* Type of Rehearsal

Memorizing the words of jokes is the most common type of rehearsal, and it is exactly what creates the performing problems I mentioned earlier. The classic rehearsal mistake beginning comics make is to reduce a funny story about something that really happened to them to the things that were said, and then memorize those words verbatim. The problem is that a very large part of what makes a joke funny lies in how the comedian *responds* to the circumstances of the story. When the comic memorizes, remembers, and finally says the words that tell the story, it's no longer in his mind in the form of pictures, sounds, and feelings. *The story loses its impact and humor because the comic has stopped responding to it as an experience.*

This problem is further exacerbated by ignorant teachers who insist you memorize the exact words of your jokes. Since the mind normally remembers in pictures, sounds, and feelings, memorizing the words violates its natural function. Then these teachers compound the difficulty by telling you to "act natural" while reciting what you have memorized. Demanding that students act natural while doing something *unnatural* puts them in a terrible double bind.

And there's another problem. Memorizing words is a process of talking to yourself in your head, repeating the words over and over until you can remember and recite them exactly. Therefore, when a comic who uses this approach gets on stage and needs to recall his memorized routine, he must go into his head and say the words to himself before repeating them to the audience. He's so busy talking to himself he doesn't establish a strong relationship with the audience, and without that he can't gather the information it takes to interpret the material in a way that will make them laugh. The jokes may be perfectly said, but they won't be funny.

Yet another problem with memorizing the words is that it leads to *emotional disassociation.* Since words don't activate behaviors, they don't activate emotions either. And emotions are the ultimate communication link between you and your audience. If you're emotionally disassociated, your audience will be, too. They've come to ride a roller coaster of your emotional ups and downs on the tracks of laughter, not to listen to a series of well-memorized words. It's not entertaining or amusing to watch someone remember and correctly repeat memorized words.

Even if you do remember your words correctly, they still aren't a very effective means of communication. The following is the work of University of California at Los Angeles professor Dr. Albert Mehrabian, published in *Silent Messages* (New York: Wadsworth, 1971), and it demonstrates the relative effectiveness of the three ways we communicate:

Body Language 55 percent

Vocal Tone 38 percent

Words 7 percent

That's right, words account for only 7 percent of our communication. We communicate 93 percent of our information with our body language and voice tone. So memorizing and repeating the words of jokes is incredibly ineffective in comparison to responding to experiences, which activate our body language and vocal tone.

You might be saying, "But in stand-up comedy words are more important than that." Great. Let's more than double the value of words and make it 15 percent. That still leaves 85 percent of the communication to body language and vocal tone. No matter how you carve it up, these nonverbal cues are far more important to communication than words.

Now I hear you asking, "But if you aren't supposed to memorize the words, how do you remember your material?"

Memorizing *Experiences* Is the *Best* Type of Rehearsal

This isn't as difficult as it might seem—you've been doing it your entire life. Do you have a story, probably one about your family or friends, that you've told many times? Did you memorize the words of that story before telling it? Of course not. You remember it as an experience.

The goal of my Rehearsal Process is to get your stand-up comedy show as vividly in your mind as that familiar story. If you want to replicate your natural sense of humor on stage, you must remember material *in the form of experiences*.

You'll derive many benefits from remembering your show as pictures, sounds, and feelings. The experiences in your routine will have an impact on your body language, voice tone, and other behaviors, which will help keep your show interesting. You'll be emotionally associated, so the audience will have the opportunity to ride your emotional roller coaster. And, with your attention focused on the audience, you'll be able to interpret your jokes in a way that will make them laugh. Does this guarantee your show will be funny? Absolutely not. But at least you won't be screwing up what you do naturally.

"But," you may say, "sometimes I need to say things in a particular way." That's fine. Just because I'm asking you to memorize experiences doesn't mean you can't say things in a particular way. Actually, some jokes require very specific phrasing. You have to learn to recall pictures, sounds, and feelings in a fashion that allows you to respond with that particular phrasing, just as you do when you're telling a personal story.

Turning sensory information into language is a very normal process. For instance, you're able to describe where you live with a specific word—*house, apartment, condo, mobile home*. You do it by picturing the place you live in your head and responding with the word that describes it. If you were to examine a picture of the place where you live, you'd find it filled with millions of details: paint, trim, windows, glass, steps, doors, doorbell, doorknob, trees, leaves, branches, grass, weeds, a garden, flowers, dirt, a sidewalk, a Jehovah's Witness, and on and on. How do you look at that picture with all those details and say the word *house? Because you've practiced.* You've rehearsed for as long as you've lived at that location. My Rehearsal Process is based on the same principle. It's easy to say exactly what you want to say if you practice responding properly to the experience.

Within Every Joke Is an Experience

This is the crux of my Rehearsal Process. A joke is a comic response to some experience, so if you know what that experience is, you can recall it as a means of remembering the joke. For instance, a student, Chekesha Showers, wrote this joke in response to her home life:

> I'm a single mom with three teenagers at home, so the subject of running away often comes up. But *I* don't.

It's the experience which resides within this joke that prompted Chekesha to think of it in the first place. If she wants to perform it with the same emotional, vocal, and physical interpretation she used when she first thought of it, she must remember those same experiences. Just memorizing the words won't activate all of the behaviors.

It's relatively easy for Chekesha to identify the experiences within this joke because it's based on events in her life. But what if you have a joke that's based on an experience that *hasn't* happened to you? Then you need to discern the experience within that joke before you can truly perform it to its maximum effect. For instance, here's an old joke I read in a joke book.

> There should be a law requiring bar stools to come with seat belts.

The experience within this joke is about someone who has gotten drunk and fallen off a bar stool so often that he figures out a solution for his problem—a seat belt. What if you don't drink? What if you've never fallen off a bar stool? If the experience has never happened to you? The first thing you must do is define the experience so you can go about remembering it as an experience.

Acting Out the POVs

My Rehearsal Process transforms your material into an experience that happens to you *in the rehearsal*. This is done by physically getting up and acting out all of the relevant POVs within an experience. When you rehearse the experience by playing out all three basic POVs, it not only happens to you as Self POV but also as any relevant Character POVs, and then Narrator POV gets to observe and make comments. Using multiple perspectives in this way gives you a kind of holographic memory of the whole experience. Now, isn't that more exciting than memorizing words?

Whatever State You're in, the Audience Is in

The audience has come to a comedy show because they want to leave their own reality and be entertained by entering someone else's. So they will naturally follow you into whatever state you are in as the means of entering your reality. It doesn't matter whether it's a positive or negative state; if you are in it, they will follow. If you play with them, they will play with you. If you blame them for not laughing, they'll blame you for not being funny. If you're emotional, they're emotional. If you don't relate to them, they won't relate to you. If you memorize the words and repeat your jokes, they will observe you saying the words of your jokes.

When You Remember and Communicate Your Material as a Sensory Experience—the Audience Will Enter Your Movie

Telling a joke versus communicating your material as a sensory experience have two profoundly different affects on an audience. If you just memorize the words of your jokes and repeat them, the audience will observe you telling them jokes. Conversely, if you remember and relate your show as a sensory experience, the audience will see, hear, and feel many of the same things you're experiencing. Both approaches get laughs, but the personal impact on the minds of the audience is the difference between being *told about something* and *living the illusion of actually being there*.

Here's a perfect example of what I mean by the illusion of actually being there. Recently, I reviewed a Bill Cosby comedy concert video, *Bill Cosby: Himself*. From a previous viewing, I remembered a scene I particularly enjoyed where Mr. Cosby makes fun of people who work hard all week, then party so much on the weekend that they make themselves sick and miserable. I vividly recalled that this scene took place in a light-colored bathroom with a toilet, a shower, a sink with a mirror, a frosted window, green towels, and so on. In the bit, Mr. Cosby was on his knees having just thrown up into the toilet. Then, he rolled his head on the porcelain and thanked it for being cold. This is how I remember that scene. On reviewing the tape this time, I was flabbergasted that Mr. Cosby acted out this scene on an empty stage using only a chair. Why did I recall all those sensory details about the bathroom? The answer is simple—Mr. Cosby memorizes the experiences of his material, then remembers and lives inside them as if they are real. As a result, I enter his movie and see, hear, and feel all of the things he does. Whatever state he is in, I am in.

The only way for you to bring the audience into your movie is for you to rehearse your material as a sensory experience, remember it as a sensory experience, and communicate it as a sensory experience. Then, and only then, can the audience perceive it as a sensory experience. This and only this opens the gateless gate through which your audience can immerse itself in your reality. Ultimately, what I want you to understand is stand-up is not a presentation, but rather an interpersonal communication of *bringing the audience into the comedy movie of your show*. But before you can do this, you must first learn to rehearse it as an experience.

8

Greg Dean's Rehearsal Process

Now that I've explained my reasons for designing this Rehearsal Process, I'd like to introduce you to it. It consists of three phases: *preparation*, *enacting the experience*, and *performing the material* based on remembering the experience.

The steps are marked to signal whether you should be in your Critic Spot(❒) or your Rehearsal Space (○). As you go through the steps, look for these symbols and move accordingly.

Phase One: Preparation
Designate a Critic Spot (❒) and a Rehearsal Space (○)

❒ Choose a joke or routine to rehearse

❒ Identify the experience that inspired the joke: "What experience would have happened in order for me to respond with this joke?"

❒ Explore the details of the experience: "Who is or is implied to be in this experience?" "Where is this experience taking place?"

❒ Decide how to enact the experience: "How do I want to enact this experience?"

Phase Two: Enact the Experience
○ Portray Self POV: "What role did I play within this experience?"

❒ Evaluate: "Did I enact my role in a way that allows me to respond with this joke?"

○ Portray Character POV: "How did other person(s) or thing(s) within this experience behave?"

❒ Evaluate: "Did I portray Character POV in a way that allows me to respond with this joke?"

○ Portray Narrator POV: "How do I want to describe what happened?"

❒ Evaluate: "Have I played all of the POVs in a way that allows me to respond with this joke?"

Phase Three: Practice Performing

❐ Decide how to communicate the experience: "How do I want to portray the POVs to perform this joke?"

○ Perform the joke or routine

❐ Evaluate the performance: "Did I communicate the experience concisely and still keep the joke structure?"

This may seem like a great deal to cover, but don't worry, like the other techniques described in this book, these steps are much simpler to do than explain. Once you understand how it all fits together, you'll whiz through your rehearsals and, in the process, acquire a vivid, long-lasting sensory memory of the material from several multiple perspectives.

Let's Rehearse

Your goal in rehearsing is *turning your material into sensory experiences from all relevant POVs as though it is actually happening to you.* You can then remember your show as you would a story about a real experience you had. The effect this will have on your audience is they will not just watch you tell jokes, but enter the movie of your show.

Unlike my other techniques described previously, this Rehearsal Process is not a step-by-step procedure, but rather a series of interactive phases. It requires you to evaluate the experience within the joke and then decide, based on that evaluation, how to enact the experience and perform the joke. To do this you may need to move back and forth between the steps as a means of coding the experience in such a manner that will make it easy for you to respond with the joke.

Feel free to customize this process. For instance, the steps have questions that are designed to help you get to the core of each step, but if different questions work better for you, by all means use them. Also there may be some step you'll need to repeat or eliminate. Since the POVs can be different for every experience, you may have to tailor it to each individual joke or routine.

Phase One: Preparation

Designate a Critic Spot (❒) And a Rehearsal Space (◯)

Define one area in the room as your Critic Spot ❒ and choose a different area to be your Rehearsal Space ◯. Physically moving between the two locations as you go through the steps of the process will help you make the necessary mental shifts between the critical and creative sides of your brain.

It's important to be sure your Critic Spot is located off to the side or even a little behind your Rehearsal Space. *Never place your Critic Spot in front of your Rehearsal Space.* If your Rehearsal Space faces your Critic Spot, you'll be practicing with a vision of your Critic located where the audience would sit. The purpose of rehearsing these two functions separately is to set the Critic aside when you're performing. To do this, the Critic Spot must be out of your sight when you're rehearsing. So place it to your right or your left or even behind you, but *never in front of you.*

❒ Choose a Joke or Routine to Rehearse

You should always be in your Critic Spot when you're analyzing something because it's an act of crafting rather than creativity. Here's the joke:

> After hearing me trash the post office, a postal worker said to me, "You shouldn't insult us." I said, "Why not?" He said, "Because we know where you live."

Since this joke isn't about something that happened to you, it will make a good demonstration of how you can make something "happen" to you in rehearsal.

❒ Identify the Experience That Inspired the Joke: "What experience would have happened in order for me to respond with this joke?"

This is the crux of the entire process, so take a little extra time to really understand it. Once you get the hang of it, the rest of the steps will be easy.

The purpose of this step is to identify the experience within the joke. As you search, you will find within every joke an implied world filled with people, animals, objects, relationships, conflicts, psychologies, environments, events, and histories all coming together to cause a moment of humor. To truly communicate the comedy within this joke you must first understand what is happening within this mini-universe. You can best do this by asking the step's question and any other questions you deem appropriate.

Q: What experience would have happened in order for me to respond with this joke?
A: A postal worker who hates his job overhears me venting my frustration about the incompetent service and warns me against saying such things. Indignant, I ask why. He threatens me with the fact that everyone at the post office has access to my address.

Is this the only experience that might have inspired this joke? For this particular joke, any other interpretation would probably be pretty similar, but some jokes can have widely divergent interpretations. Any explanation you come up with is fine as long as it's logically viable and doesn't violate the humor of the joke.

Many people go wrong at this point because they include a lot of irrelevant information in their answer. Your answer should be as concise as possible. Also notice this isn't just a description of an emotional response. For instance, I didn't just say, "I am upset." It's true that I am upset, but the experience of the incompetent service and the exchange with the postal worker are the events that upset me. An emotion is a response to an experience.

❏ EXPLORE THE DETAILS OF THE EXPERIENCE: "WHO IS OR IS IMPLIED TO BE IN THIS EXPERIENCE?" "WHERE IS THIS EXPERIENCE TAKING PLACE?" Once you've identified the experience within the joke, you'll need to uncover more specific pieces of information to use in your enactment in Phase Two. Asking the step's questions will help you do this.

Q: Who is or is implied to be in this experience?
A: A male postal worker and me.

There is nothing in this joke to indicate the postal worker's sex, but I identified the character as a male because men seem to be the ones who shoot other postal workers. If you think it would be funnier with a woman in the role, you should change it. It's also possible to give the Self POV role to another character and do the joke with two Character POVs.

Q: Where is this experience taking place?
A: In a long line at the post office.

The thing about knowing where the experience takes place is that it always has an impact on the tone of your performance. Everyone acts differently depending on whether they're at the beach, in an elevator, a restaurant, or at home. Knowing where your experience is taking place sets a context for deciding how you and your Character POVs will behave.

❐ DECIDE HOW TO ENACT THE EXPERIENCE: "HOW DO I WANT TO ENACT THIS EXPERIENCE?"
Next, put all of this information together and decide how to go about acting out the experience. This is when you need to use your imagination to mentally organize the entire experience so you can easily enact it in Phase Two.

Q: How do I want to enact this experience?
A: The *first* time I go into the Rehearsal Space, I'll be myself as Self POV and listen to the postal worker warn me not to insult postal workers. I'll ask "Why not?" and then listen to him say, "Because we know where you live." The *second* time I go into the Rehearsal Space, I'll portray the Character POV of the postal worker overhearing me insult the post office. Then he'll warn the Self POV by saying, "You shouldn't insult postal workers"; he'll listen to Self POV respond, "Why not?" then react with, "Because we know where you live." The *third* time I go into the Rehearsal Space, I'll become Narrator POV and describe the whole scene.

Your job is to create an experience so you can recall the pictures, sounds, and feelings that will allow you to respond with this joke. The only right way is *your* way.

That's all there is to Phase One. It's somewhat complicated to read about, but it only takes a minute or two of actual time to do. Now that you understand what's going on within the joke, let's move on to Phase Two, where you'll rehearse it by enacting the experience.

Phase Two: Enact the Experience

In Phase Two, you'll physically act out the experience from all of the relevant POVs so you can remember it as pictures, sounds, and feelings.

Note: The order of Phase Two is only a suggested order. Since the example joke consists of all three POVs, the following order will probably work just fine. But what if there are several Character POVs and a Narrator POV, but no Self POV? Then you must customize Phase Two to accommodate that experience.

Another note: For most people, Narrator POV will be enacted last. Since its function is that of observer, doing the Self and Character POVs first gives the Narrator POV the material it needs to fulfill its role.

One more note: When you're in the Critic Spot ❐ reviewing what you've just done in the Rehearsal Space ◯, there are four means of recalling it: Use your *imagination*, listen to an *audio tape*, review a *videotape*, or rely on the *observation of another person*. Try them all, then pick the medium that works best for you.

◯ PORTRAY SELF POV: "WHAT ROLE DID I PLAY WITHIN THIS EXPERIENCE?"
Stepping out of the Critic Spot, move into the Rehearsal Space and act out your part, Self POV, in this experience. To assist you in pinpointing how to behave in this experience, ask the step's question.

Q: What role did I play within this experience?
A: I listen to a postal worker warn me with, "You shouldn't insult postal workers." I reply, "Why not?" I listen to the postal worker say, "Because we know where you live."

It's very important you take the time to *listen* to the Character POV. I know it's kind of weird, but you'll find that the Character POV will hold up its end of the conversation.

❐ EVALUATE: "DID I ENACT MY ROLE IN A WAY THAT ALLOWS ME TO RESPOND WITH THIS JOKE?"
Back in your Critic Spot, let your Critic take over and give you feedback about whether you've played Self POV as if you were really there and if you said the right things. Ask the step's question:

Q: Did I enact my role in a way that allows me to respond with this joke?
A: Yes, I feel as if I were there and responded naturally.

If you don't like what you've done or think there was something missing, go back into your Rehearsal Space and reenact Self POV again.

○ PORTRAY CHARACTER POV: "HOW DID OTHER PERSON(S) OR THING(S) WITHIN THIS EXPERIENCE BEHAVE?"
To help you get into the experience, ask the step's question.

Q: How did other person(s) or thing(s) within this experience behave?
A: I'll portray the Character POV of the postal worker overhearing the Self POV insult the post office; then he'll warn by saying, "You shouldn't insult postal workers"; he'll listen to Self POV respond, "Why not?" then react with, "Because we know where you live."

Now go into the Rehearsal Space and act out the Character POV of the postal worker. It's the same scene, but from a different perspective. Keep the enactment real and concise. No need to give yourself a reason to babble. When you're done, go to the next step.

❒ EVALUATE: "DID I PORTRAY CHARACTER POV IN A WAY THAT AL-LOWS ME TO RESPOND WITH THIS JOKE?"
Once you're out of the experience, you can decide whether or not you've acted out the Character POVs in such a way as to preserve the joke structure. Ask the step's question to evaluate whether or not you've achieved this outcome.

Q: Did I portray Character POV in a way that allows me to respond with this joke?
A: Yes. I, as the postal worker, heard the Self POV trash the post of-fice, then warned him. I listened to his response and replied that all postal workers have access to his address.

If the answer is no, go back into the Rehearsal Space and reenact it until you feel the experience unfolds in a way that would allow you to respond with this joke.

○ PORTRAY NARRATOR POV: "HOW DO I WANT TO DESCRIBE WHAT HAPPENED?"

Narrator POV speaks directly to the audience. So when you're rehearsing, pretend there's an audience in front of you. To get a line on how to describe the previous enactments, ask the question:

Q: How do I want to describe what happened?
A: I'll say that a postal worker overheard me say something insulting and say, not as, but for the postal worker, "You shouldn't insult postal workers." Then explain how I asked him, "Why not?" and how he responded with, "Because we know where you live."

Go into the Rehearsal Space as Narrator POV and describe the interaction between the Self and the Character POV, but don't act them out. Also, if any wiseass comments come to mind, toss them in. Remember, Narrator POV isn't directly involved in the scene but is still emotionally associated and has opinions; they're just formed from a perspective of being on the outside looking in.

You've now played out the entire joke as an experience from three different POVs. Let's find out what the Critic has to say.

❐ EVALUATE: "HAVE I PLAYED ALL OF THE POVs IN A WAY THAT ALLOWS ME TO RESPOND WITH THIS JOKE?"

Back in the Critic Spot, see if you've covered all of the elements necessary for this joke to work. By now you should have the entire joke coded in your mind in the form of pictures, sounds, and feelings. Kinda cool. To figure out how to improve it, ask the question:

Q: Have I played all of the POVs in a way that allows me to respond with this joke?
A: I believe so. I acted out Self POV and Character POV accurately enough so when I was Narrator POV I was able to tell the story and keep the joke structure.

If you were able to describe what was going on from Narrator POV, and it came out with the integrity of the joke intact, you're doing your job correctly. If there were pieces missing, make note of them, go back into the Rehearsal Space, and enact them so they'll be in the experience. Then when you become Narrator POV, you'll be able to describe them. Also, notice if important words were left out. Once you identify which elements need revamping, fixing them is easy.

Phase Three: Practice Performing

The purpose of this section is to practice performing the material by remembering the pictures, sounds, and feelings of the experience. The entire experience is now in your mind and body because you've lived it by enacting it from all three POVs. The challenge is to trust that remembering the experience will prompt you to respond with this joke.

Note: If your main concern is saying the words of the joke correctly, you'll conjure up a picture of the words or say them to yourself in your head—which is exactly what I'm teaching you to avoid. Your natural sense of humor has always been expressed as a response to experiences. If you put yourself into the experience, you'll be able to remember the joke and respond with it.

A few words of caution: This Rehearsal Process has many benefits and solves most performing problems, but there's one big downside—*BABBLE*. Because you're responding to pictures with millions of details, including a myriad of sounds and a plethora of feelings, it's possible to get lost in this sensory environment and never get to the joke. This is where practice comes in. The first few performances, it's okay to babble. In your Critic Spot, you can notice the extraneous chatter and decide what you should focus on to help you get to the joke.

The freedom to allow yourself to babble is a doubled-edged sword. It can be positive because exploring all the little details within the experience can help you discover new jokes. But if you're trying to rehearse a specific show and want to get to the joke without mentioning all those superfluous details, babble can be a real problem.

My suggestion is to first get to the joke without babbling. Once you've accomplished that, then explore.

❏ DECIDE HOW TO COMMUNICATE THE EXPERIENCE: "HOW DO I WANT TO PORTRAY THE POVS TO PERFORM THIS JOKE?"
Spend some time figuring out how you want to perform this joke. Do you want to act out the Self and Character POVs? Or do you want to tell the story entirely from Narrator POV? Or use a combination of

both? You're not stuck with any one choice; you can try it several different ways. But always begin with a specific strategy. You can do this by asking the question:

Q: How do I want to portray the POVs to perform this joke?
A: I'll start from Narrator POV to describe how a postal worker overheard me, then step into the position of the Character POV of the postal worker and say, "You shouldn't insult postal workers." Then I'll step back to the place where Self POV was standing and reply, "Why not?" then shift back into the postal worker and say, "Because we know where you live."

○ PERFORM THE JOKE OR ROUTINE
It's now a simple matter of going into the Rehearsal Space and practicing communicating the experience by remembering the pictures, sounds, and feelings. Remember, how you rehearse is how you will perform, so have fun while you're rehearsing.

In writing about a practice performance it's impossible for me to describe all of the comedian's funny behavioral responses, but I want to mention that they're a major by-product of this kind of preparation. To help me fill this in, imagine you're performing the jokes. Here's a rendition of how this joke might go.

Narrator POV: Yesterday, I was in a long line at the post office bitching about the service and a postal worker overheard me. He said,
Character POV: "You really shouldn't insult us like that."
Self POV: "Oh yeah, why not?"
Character POV: "Because we know where you live."

Notice the phrasing has altered somewhat. Always feel free to phrase things as you or the Character POV would say because the joke should come as an honest response to the experience. If you're trying to match the exact wording of the original joke, you've missed the whole point of my Rehearsal Process.

❐ EVALUATE THE PERFORMANCE: "DID I CONCISELY COMMUNICATE THE EXPERIENCE AND STILL KEEP THE JOKE STRUCTURE?"
This evaluation is pivotal to the quality of your show. It's where you're going to decide if the joke is tight enough, if you've kept it in joke

form, and if you like your performance. A helpful evaluation tool is the step's question:

Q: Did I concisely communicate the experience and still keep the joke structure?
A: The joke makes sense and I've kept the joke structure, though I could trim it down a little bit.

If you don't like what you've done, *do it again*. If you like what you've done, *do it again*. If you're not sure, *do it again*. Once you've done it again, *do it again*. Practice responding to the experience so you can perform the material as if it were something that actually happened to you. Which it did—in the rehearsal.

If you have other questions of your own, ask them: Did I like my performance? Did I babble? Did I keep the integrity of the joke? Do I think it's funny? Can I give the punch to another POV to make it funnier? If you're dissatisfied with any aspect of your performance, ponder those changes, then go back into your Rehearsal Space and reenact the POVs or just try another performance. If you like what you've done, repeat it a couple of times to get a handle on it. I've discovered performing the material several times helps me express it in the way that's true for me.

Babble is the enemy. Even though you've got a wealth of information you can see, hear, and feel, you've got to learn to focus on what will help you get to the joke. Here's a version with too much babble:

Narrator POV: Yesterday, maybe the day before, it doesn't matter—anyway, I was in a long line at the post office. I was there to get some stamps and check my post office box. I hate the post office, and I start saying all kinds of bad things about it, when this postal worker overhears what I'm saying. He doesn't like it, so he decides to come over and tell me what he thinks. He says to me . . .
Character POV: "Ya know, we work really hard and I resent the nasty things you're saying about postal workers and you really shouldn't say those kinds of things. You know what I mean?"
Narrator POV: So, I said to him . . .
Self POV: "No, I don't know what you mean. I can say anything I want to say. It's a free country. And why shouldn't I?"

117

Character POV: "Because everyone who hears you insult them has access to your address, so they know where you live."

It's the same experience, but with too much description. Not only does this lengthen the joke, it messes up the structure. From what I've witnessed in my classes, this is actually mild babble. I've had students who can turn a one-liner into a novella.

If you've come up with some new jokes, you'll want to think about how to work them into the bit. Go to the Rehearsal Space to insert them into the experience. Once you're satisfied with the performance, rehearse something else.

There's my Rehearsal Process in a nutshell. Okay, so it's a huge nutshell. Just a few pages short of *War and Peace*. But well worth the journey, because in this chapter you've learned to code the experience of a joke in pictures, sounds, and feelings instead of memorizing the words. You've also learned how to separate your Creator from your Critic and acquired a format for rehearsing them separately so your performance can be free of self-criticism. And you've learned to enact the experience of your material from multiple POVs. Applying all of this new knowledge will allow your mind and, hence, your sense of humor to operate naturally so you can be the funny person you already are by getting the audience to enter your comedy movie.

Now it's your turn. Using the Rehearsal Process Worksheet, rehearse the five jokes at the bottom of the form.

Rehearsal Process Worksheet

Use or *don't* use whatever you need to turn the below *jokes* into *sensory experiences* which will actually happen to you during your rehearsal.

Phase One: Preparation
Designate a Critic Spot (❐) and a Rehearsal Space (O)
❐ Choose a Joke or Routine to Rehearse
❐ Identify the Experience that Inspired the Joke: "What experience would have happened in order for me to respond with this joke?"
❐ Explore the Details of the Experience: "Who is or is implied to be in this experience?" "Where is this experience taking place?"
❐ Decide How to Enact the Experience: "How do I want to enact this experience?"

Phase Two: Enact The Experience
O Portray Self POV: "What role did I play within this experience?"
❐ Evaluate: "Did I enact my role in a way that allows me to respond with this joke?"
O Portray Character POV: "How did other person(s) or thing(s) within this experience behave?"
❐ Evaluate: "Did I portray Character POV in a way that allows me to respond with this joke?"
O Portray Narrator POV: "How do I want to describe what happened?"
❐ Evaluate: "Have I played all of the POVs in a way that allows me to respond with this joke?"

Phase Three: Practice Performing
❐ Decide How to Communicate the Experience: "How do I want to portray the POVs to perform this joke?"
O Perform the Joke or Routine
❐ Evaluate the Performance: "Did I communicate the experience concisely and still keep the joke structure?"

Plug the Below Jokes into the Rehearsal Process
I was standing in line at Ralph's so long that the kid on the milk carton had been found.
Every man should have a wife—preferably his own.
Inside of every short person is a tall person all hunched over.
My friends all say I'm paranoid . . . well I didn't actually *hear* them say it.
The baby sitter wants to know where you keep your fire extinguisher.

9

Microphone Technique
Dos and Don'ts

Having no experience with a microphone can be an ordeal for the beginner's first times on stage. At first the mike will seem like this awkward phallus with an annoying cord that's always underfoot, but with a few tips and a little practice, using it will become second nature. In fact, you'll soon come to depend on it because controlling an audience is so much easier when you're louder than they can ever be.

My suggestion is to use something to simulate a microphone while rehearsing so you can get comfortable holding something in your hands while performing. Reportedly, my students have employed large spoons, hairbrushes, and a stick with rope tied to it. You'll know you have good microphone technique when it becomes virtually invisible to you and the audience.

Here are some basic *dos* and *don'ts* for using a hand mike on stage in a nightclub.

When Entering the Stage

- *DON'T* leave the mike in the stand for your entire show.
- *DO* take the mike out of the stand at the beginning of your show and place the stand at the back of the stage. The rule of thumb is: Hold the mike in your hand unless the bit requires your hands to be free; only then put it back on the stand.

If the Microphone Doesn't Work

- *DON'T* pound the mike into your hand.
- *DO* check to see if the on button is turned to on.
- *DON'T* twist the jack at the bottom of the mike. The jack con-

necting the cord to the mike has prongs that can be bent by twisting, which will permanently damage the mike and the jack.

- DO push the jack further into the bottom of the mike to make a better connection.
- DON'T yank on the cord. You could very easily pull the wires loose in the cord or the jack that plugs into the wall.
- DO test the jack at the end of the cord that plugs into the wall or side of the stage.

If It Still Doesn't Work

- DON'T get angry, throw a fit, or put down the club for having bad equipment. It just makes you look amateurish.
- DO politely let the manager know that the P.A. system isn't working. Then put the mike in the stand, set it aside, raise your voice, and do your show to the best of your ability.

If The Mike Works But You Can't Hear Yourself

- DON'T yell really loud as a joke. If the mike *is* on you'll hurt the audience's ears or possibly blow out a speaker. Either way, you'll look like a jerk.
- DO speak a little louder, gradually raising your voice until you can hear yourself. Or ask the audience if they can hear you. It's not as important that you can hear yourself as it is that *they* can hear you. There are what I call *deaf stages*, where the speakers are so far in front of the proscenium that the performers on stage can't hear themselves at all, although the audience can hear just fine.

How to Hold a Mike

- DON'T cover the lower portion of your face with the mike.
- DO hold the mike so it could graze the bottom of your chin.
- DON'T speak directly into the mike. It distorts the sound, and the breathy consonants—P, B, F, and W—will make whooshing or popping sounds.
- DO speak over the top of the mike. Most hand mikes are omnidirectional, which means they pick up sound just as well from any

angle within a certain distance. Holding the mike at chin level, you'll easily be within that distance.

In Dealing with the Cord

- *DON'T* walk directly into the cord. It'll ride up between your legs. Then, when you turn around, it might wrap around one leg.
- *DO* gently flip the cord toward the audience so that it hangs away from your body and you can walk about the stage unencumbered.
- *DON'T* keep kicking the cord out of your way. The audience will be watching your foot instead of listening to your comedy.
- *DO* use your foot occasionally to push the cord out in front of you.
- *DON'T* step on the cord while walking. You could tear the mike out of your hand and/or damage the jack or cord.
- *DO* take the time to look down to see where the cord is.
- *DON'T* gather the cord up in your microphone hand. When you reach the end of the cord while walking, besides looking like an idiot, you could pop the cord and mike right out of your hand or the wall.
- *DO* let the cord hang down in front of you. It will seem odd at first, but you'll quickly become accustomed to it. Again, if you keep the cord toward the audience, it'll hang away from your body.
- *DON'T* wind the cord around the wrist of your free hand.
- *DO* leave your free hand available for gesturing.
- *DON'T* stroke up and down on the cord; it will appear as if you're masturbating.
- *DO* allow your hand to rest at your side when you're not gesturing.

When Gesturing

- *DON'T* gesture with the hand that's holding the mike. Your hand and the mike will move away from your mouth and the audience won't hear what you're saying.
- *DO* gesture with the non-mike hand. Feel free to transfer the mike from hand to hand as your need to gesture changes.

When Adjusting the Mike Stand

- *DON'T* loosen the center tightener all the way when adjusting the height of the mike stand. If you forget which direction to turn it, you can easily spend a full minute trying to get the stand to tighten up again.

- *DO* loosen the tightener slightly, step on the bottom of the stand to stabilize it, adjust, then tighten. If it doesn't tighten quickly, you're going in the wrong direction.
- *DON'T* take time to adjust the stand to just the perfect height and then take the mike out of it and set it behind you.
- *DO* take the mike out immediately and place the stand out of the way.

Coping with the Unexpected

- *DON'T* ignore accidents and mistakes such as the mike holder coming off in your hand, knocking over the stand, wrapping the cord around your leg, or any other unforeseen event.
- *DO* acknowledge what's happening, then deal with it: Put the mike holder back on the stand, set the mike stand back up, or unwrap the cord from your leg. If you don't attend to the problem, the audience will stare at it until you do.

When Leaving the Stage

- *DON'T* put the mike on a table or the floor.
- *DO* put it back in the mike stand. It's the mike stand's only job.
- *DON'T* toss the mike to the M.C.
- *DO* hand it to the M.C. if he's right there at the end of your show.
- *DON'T* turn the mike off because the M.C. will speak immediately upon receiving it.
- *DO* practice all of the above DOs, and you'll look and sound like a professional comedian.

10

Peak Performance

Performing stand-up comedy is an extraordinarily complex matter. There are so many nuances and subtleties you can only learn from performing. You'll quickly discover that performing is not just performing. It's also a means of facing your personal demons, a trek into the unknown, a chance to practice, an opportunity to experiment, a form of expression, and a way of getting your rocks off by making people laugh.

Here are some secrets, tips, and guidelines about performing that will help to make the most of your comic journey.

SECRET #11:
YOUR JOB IS TO BE FUNNY.

Many beginners and even some pros mistakenly believe their job is to *just* do their show as written no matter what. Not true. Your job as a funny person is to be funny. If you can accomplish this by doing your show, great. But what if your show isn't working? That's when you'll need to be creative and adventurous enough to ferret out what will make the audience laugh.

There are always options for making people laugh if you're willing to take the risks that go with searching for them. Many of the suggestions in this chapter are designed to give you those options. Some of them you can use right away, others you'll have to practice. All of them will come into play at some point in your career as a professional comedian. Decide now that your job is not just doing a show. Your job is being funny.

Comic Timing

I'd . . . timing . . . damn . . . I'd like to . . . timing . . . oops . . . I'd like to discuss a subject that I don't bel . . . timing? . . . lieve . . . shit . . . I'd like to discuss an aspect of comedy that I don't believe can be meaningfully discussed—timing. Like love, happiness, and sushi, timing defies analysis. There have been many attempts to define it, but most were futile. Years ago, in their book *How to Be a Comedian for Fun and Profit* (Lauf King Publishers, Studio City, CA, 1972), Harry King and Lee Lauger wrote, "Timing is knowing when to stop speaking in the midst of a routine in order to allow thinking time for the audience to prepare itself for the laugh that is coming up" (29). Not much of a definition, but it is a great piece of advice.

The only thing that's certain about comic timing is that it's essential to being funny. And that's why we're going to discuss it—not because it'll be meaningful, but because it'll be useful.

When discussing a subjective area such as timing, I've found that it often helps to start with a story.

Several years ago, I was studying Neuro Linguistic Programming (NLP) with its cofounder, John Grinder, and codeveloper, Judy DeLozier. Knowing NLP to be a heady subject, John and Judy wanted everyone to get their bodies involved in the learning process, so they offered a class in African dancing with live drumming.

Well, I had done a fair amount of dance, but African dancing was a new experience for me. I quickly discovered that the undulating movements, the unique rhythms, and the improvisational style of the changing steps was not a style indigenous to Caucasian people.

Feeling rather frustrated, I went to the head of this African group, Titos Sampa, and asked him for help. He said, "You're counting and trying to do the moves correctly, right?" I replied, "Right." Titos laughed and advised me, "Stop all that. Watch the lead dancer and *become* the drum." I inquired, "*Become* the drum? *Become* the drum? Americans start dancing when the band starts playing, and we stop dancing when it stops. *Become* the drum?" Titos clarified, "Feel the drum in your chest, move as the drum moves, and you'll do much better."

I tried it. It was strange, but it worked. Feeling the drum's rhythms in my chest allowed me to find these unfamiliar African movements in my body. I was astounded at the effectiveness of becoming the drum.

After several months of the African dancing, I was getting fairly good, so I decided I wanted to do some drumming. I asked Titos, and he agreed. The drumming was more difficult than the dancing. Getting one rudimentary beat took me half an hour. My biggest problem, though, was that the group of three drummers kept changing the tempo. In unison, they'd speed up or slow down for no apparent reason. I was completely flummoxed. It was as if there was some drumming muse that they were all plugged into and I wasn't even near the socket.

After that night's dancing and drumming, I asked Titos what the impetus was for the changing tempo. "Oh that, he replied. "We're following the dancers." I was flabbergasted. "Wait. Wait. The drummers are following the dancers? But when I was a dancer, you told me to become the drum. So if the dancers are following the drummers and the drummers are following the dancers, *there's no one in charge!*" A huge grin washed across Titos's face as he proclaimed, "Exactly. Now you got it." He laughed a booming laugh and walked away.

I stood in a stupor talking to myself, "I've got what?" Then it dawned on me. No one is in charge. No one is ever in charge. We all affect one another. Sometimes we're a dancer. Sometimes we're a drummer. At different times we're all leading and following. It's a loop of affecting and being affected.

My *definition of comic timing is African dancing and drumming.* The audience is following the comedian and the comedian is following the audience. The comedian doesn't *have* timing; the comedian *spontaneously creates* timing based on how he or she is being affected by the audience. You can't decide on it ahead of time because it's an act of creativity that happens in the present.

This sheds more light on the validity of the principle *the relationship with the audience is the most important thing.* If you concentrate only on doing your material just as you rehearsed it, your timing will be based on trying to repeat your rehearsal, not on how you affect the audience and how the audience affects you in the present. Each show has different timing because each show has a different audience.

This is why comedians don't like to analyze their ability to be funny. The most important ingredient is a phenomenon that cannot be defined in words. It's like the taste of a strawberry. I can describe what a strawberry tastes like from now until I die, but it won't help you understand it. The only way to know how a strawberry tastes is simply to taste one. And the only way to know comic timing is to experience it for yourself. Great comedians have comic timing, but they can't discuss it in any meaningful way because it's different every time. And though I believe that comic timing can be learned, it can't be taught. The only way you'll learn it is through trial and error. If you have it already, it's because you went through that trial and error in your childhood.

The purpose of my discussion here is simply to explain that comic timing happens in the moment, in the feedback loop between you and each individual audience. There's no need to discuss or even think about comic timing, but you will have it if you *dance with your audience*.

Tape Record Every Show

Take a tape recorder on stage and place it on the stool, table, or set it offstage in a location that's not directly in front of a house speaker. If you place it too near a speaker, it'll record your voice but not the audience's laughter. And the laughter (or silence, for that matter) is what you need to hear to gauge the effectiveness of your jokes.

Remember, when you leave the stage take your recorder with you. That may sound obvious, but you'll often be in a daze when you leave the stage, so get in the habit of grabbing your tape recorder. Or ask another comic to remind you. I can tell you from experience that comedy clubs are littered with forgotten tape recorders.

The First Show

There are as many types of first shows as there are people who have done them. But first shows usually fit one of two extreme categories, described below.

Crash and Burn
The blinding spotlight throws you off, your mind goes blank, your voice quivers, a red-hot flush sweeps over your head, sweat runs down your face, you're completely brain dead, and what jokes you can remember—bomb. Of course, this is a worst-case scenario, but I have a couple of hints that will help you pull through.

Keep in mind that you've just taken a step into the unknown. After your first show, it will no longer be a complete mystery. If you bombed, you now know that you can do poorly in front of people and survive. You'll quickly realize that if that's as bad as it gets, it's not all that bad.

Also, your lack of success could mean that you've been rehearsing the wrong way. When you forget your material, it's either because your Critic is on stage with you or the state you rehearsed in is different than the one you performed in.

Perfection

Often something magical happens with a first show. You're so scared that your unconscious mind takes over and you do an excellent show. Sometimes this can be worse than bombing. When you bomb you know there are things to work on, but if you do a perfect show, you might fool yourself into thinking you've got a handle on this very complicated art. *You don't.* Not after one performance, not after one year—maybe in three to five years.

The best performances are the ones where you hit enough to feel good and miss enough to realize you still have a lot to learn. Be careful not to get arrogant after one or two good shows. Stand-up comedy is like a wild animal; just when you think you have it under control, it'll turn around and bite you in the ass.

Prepare a Show List

A show list is a list of the jokes and bits you're planning to do in the show. Take the time to make a show list before you get to the club, using the following tips.

Use Code Words

A show list is not supposed to be a verbatim transcript. It's just to remind you of the order of your show, so use code words. Many people write their code words on an index card, but I prefer standard binder paper because I believe a show list should be an emergency measure. A visible show list is tacky, so if it's written on a large piece of paper, you'll be less likely to pull it out and refer to it during your show.

Write the Show List on Your Hand

Writing your show list on your hand has several advantages. You can't misplace it, it's convenient, and you can surreptitiously glance at it whenever you want. But, there are also a couple of pitfalls.

One of my students, Yvonne Brenner, wrote her code words on her hand, then went on stage without her glasses. She ended up making this problem very funny by asking a man in the audience to read her hand and tell her what bit to do next. The next showcase, she wrote the list on her hand again. This time she did remember to wear her spectacles, but she carried a glass of soda in the hand that had her code words on it, and the moisture from the glass erased her entire show.

Supply an Introduction

How you're brought on stage will set the tone for your show. Of course, it's best to come on with a laugh that foreshadows your particular comic slant. Since most M.C.s won't know you, supply them with an introduction that will bring you on stage the way you want.

There are some M.C.s who won't use the introduction you provide. They're going to do whatever they want. The best option here is to get to know them personally so they'll want to help you because they like you. Until then, you'll just have to live with it. You can only do what you can do.

Never Tell the M.C., "Just Say Anything."

You're assuming the M.C. is competent. Bad assumption. Especially at open mike nights, M.C.s are often control freaks who want stage time so much they're willing to run the whole evening. I began giving my own introduction to M.C.s after one introduced me as "The man who invented the blow job."

Even if you happen upon a good M.C., giving him or her permission to "just say anything" is still a bad idea. One comic I know, when he's the M.C. and people tell him this, will purposely mess with them just to teach them a lesson. Here is a paraphrase of one of his "educational" introductions:

> Our next dickhead is a knuckle dragging mouth-breather, who made a big mistake when he entered the club tonight. He told me

he was going to get more laughs than the other comics because this audience would laugh at anything since you have the I.Q. of a cuff link. You can make up your mind whether you think he's right or not—here's Joe Blow."

It was a comedy nightmare. After the show, the comic blew up at the M.C., but the M.C. laughed it off, saying "You told me I could say anything. So shut up, and next time give me something."

Put Your Introduction on a Three-by-Five-Inch Index Card

This will help because the M.C. can stick it in his pocket and read it on stage. Print it in large letters that'll be easy to read. Sometimes performers go on stage without their glasses. Also, bring two or three duplicate cards because the M.C. may lose the original before it's time to bring you up. If you have an extra, you'll be able to hand it to him just before your introduction.

Spell Your Name Phonetically

If your name is difficult to pronounce, print it out phonetically. One student was blessed with the name Mark Dziwanowski, (jew-van-ow-ski). As Mark is fond of saying, "I've got consonants in my name who've never met."

If he doesn't spell his name phonetically for M.C.s, they'll either screw it up completely or just introduce him as "Mark." This is okay if you have material to deal with the recurring incident.

Make It Funny

If the M.C. thinks he'll get a laugh with it, he's more likely to use it. Here's one that I give to M.C.s because they can't screw it up:

Our next gentleman needs no introduction—(walk off stage).

The M.C. gets a laugh, and I get to introduce myself.

Use Credits

If you have some legitimate credits, put them in your introduction. But don't give the audience your resume. One or two good credits are enough. Any more than that and it'll seem as if you're trying too hard to impress the audience.

If you don't have any credits, then make fun of that with a standard like this:

If you've seen *Comic Relief, The Tonight Show,* or *An Evening At the Improv,* well, this gentleman has *seen* these shows. Here's Greg Dean."

Of course, use your own name. It'll confuse the audience if you always introduce yourself as Greg Dean.

Incorporate Your Subject Matter

You'll be ahead of the game if you're brought up with an introduction that mentions your first bit or the central theme of your show. If you're starting your show with some television material, then write an intro about being a couch potato. If you just broke up with your lover, be introduced as someone "easy to get along with." If you're a sports fan and your first bit is about sports, then try something like:

Ladies and Gentlemen, our sports fanatic for the night, Joe Blow.

It's better to have an unfunny introduction that sets you up to get into your material than to have a funny one that puts you in the wrong light.

Design It to Present Your Personality or Attributes

Not everyone will have an identity in the beginning, so this may not apply. But if you have some overt characteristic like being really fat, cranky, tall, you wear thick glasses, or are of a particular ethnic group, use it to your advantage.

For one of my short students, we wrote an intro that had the M.C. put the microphone stand all the way up, then say,

Welcome a big man in his field, Jim Ridgley.

Jim would walk out and the mike would be about a foot over his head. He'd get his first laugh just by standing and looking at the mike.

Remember, a good introduction can set the proper tone for your entire show. Just as a bad one can dig a hole that may take you some time to get out of. Introductions are important, so take the time to create one that's right for you.

Warm Up

Before a show begins, you'll want to warm up so your comedy motor will be ready for the race when you step on stage. As a beginner, you'll usually get about three to six minutes to perform. If you go on stage cold, by the time you hit your stride your time will be up.

There is no "right way" to warm up; every comedian has different needs when preparing to get in front of people and make them laugh. Here are some tips for getting physically, vocally, and psychologically warmed up.

Physical Exercise

Walk briskly. Run in place. Try doing some push ups. If that's too strenuous, do them off of a wall rather than the floor. Generally, go through your body and move and stretch. The idea is to release the stress and get physically loose.

A word of warning: Don't overdo it, otherwise you could go on stage so out of breath that the audience won't be able to understand what you're saying through the huffing and puffing.

Get into a Playful Mood

When you play around or act silly, you loosen up so your sense of humor can come forward. Try acting like a piece of bacon. Make faces. Do a goofy walk. Do part of your show as Jerry Lewis. Whatever gets you into a playful space.

When I was the opening act for male strippers at Chippendale's in Los Angeles, I did one or two shows a night, four times a week, for three-and-a-half years. Some nights it was very difficult to get up for a show, so I designed rituals that helped me get into a playful mood. First of all, putting on a costume—my tuxedo pants, vest, and cummerbund—helped change my focus from the real world to the performing world. Next, I'd play box and punch inanimate objects like a pair of pants, a hanger, a stripper's costume (though never with anyone's G-string). Then, just before going out, I'd annoy one of the dancers with my play boxing. God forbid that someone's guest should come into the dressing room at that time because I'd playfully harass them, either tickling them or punching them in the butt. When my introductory music came on, I'd march out of the dressing room, hit the steps in time with the music, turn around, walk back into the dressing room, make a face, then, doing a silly march, I'd go to the place where I waited to be introduced.

Be Quiet and Focus

Some people need to be left alone before they perform. If this is your style, physically warm up, then find a place where you can be somewhat alone. But be sure to let the M.C. know where you are—you don't want him to think you've disappeared.

I have this need to be alone, but only for sixty seconds before I go on stage. Before that I'll play and jump around, but then just as I'm ready to step on stage I go internal until I'm introduced. If someone interrupts me when I've gone inside myself, I get very cranky.

I've learned to explain my quirks to the people I work around, so they won't think I'm just being a jerk. If you let people know, they'll usually be accommodating.

Run Through Your Show

Going through your show can remind you of the order of your material, refresh your memory of new jokes, and help put you into a playful state. There are several ways of doing this, but let me start by saying that I don't recommend running silently through your show in your head. For some reason, running through a performance in your head doesn't help it come out of your mouth. You can try it, but you'll quickly learn what all actors know: The least you should do is say it out loud. Which brings up the next option, stand up and go through your show out loud. The closer you can get to the state you want to perform in, the better. My favorite is called the *hyper run-through*. This involves going through your show out loud, as fast as you can possibly speak. You'll quickly pinpoint the areas you're not completely comfortable with because you'll stumble over them.

Think Up Jokes

Some comics like to sit and think of some opening jokes for their show. They'll lampoon the M.C., the environment, or go off of the material of the previous comedians. These jokes will usually just work for that one show or maybe that one gig.

In one club, I was following a pretty redheaded lady who did material about being up all night having kinky sex with a stranger. When I entered the stage I pretended to be exhausted and proclaimed I'd been up all night having sex with a kinky redhead. It yielded a big and easy laugh.

Get on Stage During the Applause

It's tacky when the M.C. introduces you and leaves the stage and the audience applauds so long that they stop before you finally walk on stage and start your show in an uncomfortable silence. It's much better to get on stage while the audience is applauding, take the mike out of the stand, move it out of the way, and begin as the applause subsides. To time this out properly, you must know the layout of the club. Stand as near the stage as you can without distracting the audience.

Avoid Cliché Greetings

You don't want the first few words out of your mouth to be a cliché. Greet the audience like a group of friends. Say "hello" to some of them personally, wave to people in the back, talk about some of the things that went on earlier in the evening. When a comic comes out and jumps right into his act, it's often jolting. The purpose of the greeting is to familiarize yourself with the group of people in front of you and begin building a relationship. It's not an obligation you have to fulfill with some annoying cliché. If you talk to the audience you might be surprised to find out that there are people out there.

To learn how annoying these clichés can get, sit in a comedy club audience some time, and after the tenth or eleventh comic in a row that starts their show with. . .

Hi. How you all doin' tonight?

. . . you'll want to scream, "We're fine. Just stop asking us that!" And there's also this overused ditty:

Are you enjoying the show so far?

And the newest hack phrase:

Wus up?

The audience just wants to enjoy the show and not be forced to applaud or answer out loud because every comic in the lineup has the same hackneyed greeting. They'll enjoy the show a lot more if the comedians are original.

Develop a Strong Opening Line

After you greet the audience, it'll help you to relax if your first shot at being funny gets a big laugh. So having a great opening joke really helps. It can also establish who you are.

For example, a black student, Carol McGrath, starts her show by standing at the mike, giving the audience time to observe her, and then says:

As you can tell by looking at me, I'm Canadian.

Another student, Mel McKee, capitalizes on the fact that he's a mature man in a club filled with mostly young people. He opens with:

I wake up almost every morning.

Acknowledge the Obvious

If there's something about you the audience might fixate on, you must address it so they'll let it go and you can get on with your show. The kind of things I'm talking about are usually physical, but they can also be personality traits. For instance, if you are obese, have one crossed eye, your national origin is unclear, you have a physical tic or a missing or deformed limb, these things need to be addressed so the audience can relax and enjoy your comedy instead of wondering about these anomalies.

It's not always a physical attribute that needs to be acknowledged; sometimes it's a personality trait. An example of this is my student Sharky. He's a very nice man, but there's something a little edgy about his manner that sometimes makes the audience uncomfortable. I suggested he broach this with a joke. He did:

If you don't like me but you like my jokes, do what you do at home—close your eyes and pretend I'm someone else.

This next example is also about one of my students, Jeff Pines. He came to my class a bit shy because he has a speech impediment. When he speaks you can understand him, but he has an obvious lisp and I felt it needed to be addressed. Preferably with a joke. I wasn't sure how Jeff would take my advice, but in class the following week Jeff began his show with this:

> Greg says I have a speech impediment. Maybe it's just that your ears are screwed up.

This was very funny because not only did he reverse the situation, he got to bag on the teacher. Well, Jeff went on to the advanced workshop where he continued to make up jokes about his lisp. Then on the joke writing night of the workshop, I mentioned that he could turn his lisp into a character. From this Speech Impediment Man was born. Every week the Speech Impediment Man routine got funnier and funnier with jokes like:

> Wherever there's a drunk who needs me to translate for him, I'll be there.

Then, during his routine on showcase night, Jeff surprised everyone by tearing open his shirt to reveal a T-shirt sporting a Superman logo with an extra *I* in the middle of it to signify Speech Impediment Man. The audience roared; I think I even heard a couple of foreheads hit the table. This is an excellent example of turning a problem into an asset through a willingness to have a sense of humor about it.

Avoid All Comics' Clichés

Notice the phrases and idiosyncracies that all the hack comics are using, and avoid them like unsafe sex. I'm not discussing societal clichés, which are fodder for material, but those stock things that will quickly transform you from a unique individual to a stereotype.

Physical Clichés

These are all those recurring habits that comics pick up from other comics. Real people don't act like this. Here are a few:

Leaning with one hand on the mike stand.

Pacing back and forth looking down at the floor.

Leaning forward into the audience to deliver a line.

Clapping your hands together between jokes.

Picking up and smacking down the mike stand to indicate a punch.

Nodding *yes* when the audience is laughing at a joke.

These aren't all of them. Each generation seems to add a few more to the ever-growing ranks of the overused and tired.

Verbal Clichés

I know I've discussed verbal comics' clichés in Chapter 4, but it's worth a second visit:

Have you ever noticed . . . ?

But seriously . . .

I don't want to say . . .

What else? What else?

What's that all about?

Especially, get rid of the verbs *love* and *hate*. Why use something so pat when there are so many alternative words for how you feel about a subject that are much more interesting? Refer to a thesaurus. Even M.C.s aren't immune to the trendy:

Give it up for—Joe Blow.

Make note of all these clichés and eliminate them from your show. The one exception to this rule is when you wish to satirize them. For instance, several of my students have started their shows by saying:

Hi. How you all doin' tonight? Why am I asking that? I don't care how you're doing. I'm fine.

Don't Ask a Question as a Segue

Of all of the comics' clichés, asking a question as a means of bringing up a new subject matter is the most frequently abused and the biggest waste of valuable stage time. It's a personal quest of mine to eradicate this mindless affectation from stand-up comedy. Watch the stand-up comedy shows on television, and count the number of times the comics use a question as a segue. It always starts with the phrase:

How many people here . . . ?

Not only is it annoying, but it requires a show of hands or an audible response from the audience. Then, the comic usually ignores the response because he isn't interested in it. He's simply trying to make a transition from one subject to another. If the comic does acknowledge the response, it's only to dismiss it so he can get into his routine. For instance, I saw a female comic who used this question as a segue to get into her routine about phobias:

How many people here have a phobia?

This drew a strong response from a lady in the back of the room, who yelled:

Oh, I do. I have a horrible fear of spiders.

Since the female comic didn't really want a response, she dismissed the lady with the spider phobia by saying,

Yeah, that's nice. I have a fear of heights.

And she went on with her routine. The audience soured on the comic because she asked them a question but then callously shut down someone who responded.

Another misguided use of this kind of question is when the comic doesn't get the response he wants but goes on with his routine anyway. When I was doing an open mike in a biker bar in southern California, the comic performing before me asked:

How many people here went to college?

In the bar there were about fifteen greasy-haired, tattooed, leather-clad, smoking, drinking, chain-from-the-pants-to-the-wallet bikers who peered at each other as if to say, "College? I hardly got through junior high." Consequently, no one raised their hand or verbally replied. Nevertheless, the comic went on with his preprogrammed set:

Great. I guess you can relate to this then.

The bikers cracked up. Not because the comic was funny, but because even these counterculture misfits recognized that he was oblivious to the nonanswer he hadn't received. Hopefully, you can understand why this is my pet peeve.

Now, for the solutions. Instead of asking a question as a segue, simply state your *negative opinion* about the subject. Our female comic could have said something like:

I have this horrendous fear of heights.

This would get her into her routine quickly without her having to parry an unwanted response. Or our college graduate could have said something like:

My college years were pure torture for me.

Riffing is one of the only appropriate reasons for asking the audience questions, because in this case you really want to develop a comedic dialogue. If you're going to ask the audience a question, be prepared to converse with those who answer. Otherwise, state your negative opinion about your subject, which will save you time and segue into your next bit.

Watch Out for the Motormouth Syndrome

The motormouth syndrome occurs when the comic goes through the material without stopping for laughs or even a breath. You're on stage to have fun making people laugh. Slow down. Enjoy yourself. Remember, stand-up comedy is a relationship with the audience, not an opportunity for target practice with a joke Uzi. Here are a couple of reasons for the motormouth syndrome and their solutions:

Fear of Forgetting Your Material

When beginners are afraid that they'll forget their material, they sometimes hurry from one joke to the next as fast as they can. This seems as if it would work, but it doesn't. Actually, you're more likely to go blank when you're just trying to get through the material because any little interruption will mix you up completely. Besides, it's not entertaining to watch someone rush through their material. The audience wants to laugh, not watch someone rush through their show because they're afraid of forgetting. The solution to this problem is to rehearse properly, take a show list on stage, have fun, and focus on your relationship with the audience.

Trying to Fit too Much Material into the Allotted Time

This is usually a result of being too greedy. I know you want to get all your best jokes into your show, but trying to cram in too much material is a self-defeating proposition. You may get more jokes in, but if you have to race through them you can't possibly perform them at their true potential. There's nothing sadder than watching a comic mess up a series of really great jokes by performing them on fast forward.

To avoid this, find out how much time you'll have on stage, and then rehearse a show at least 30 seconds shorter than the time allotted. This will give you a comfort zone, so you can have fun and play without feeling any pressure to hurry. And if you should bomb, you'll be glad you're doing a shorter show. It's better to do fewer jokes well then many jokes badly.

Perform the Setups with Equal Commitment

Many comics treat joke setups strictly as information. They relate them to the audience in an offhand manner, saving their commitment for the punch. I think this is a big mistake for several reasons. First of all, the setup constitutes 95 to 99 percent of most jokes, which means most comics spend around 95 to 99 percent of their time onstage doing setups. Choosing to simply rattle them off is a terrible waste of valuable stage time. Secondly, it's your performance of the setup that causes the audience to accept your target assumption. If the setup is merely reported, this misdirection won't be as effective and the punch won't have as much impact. Give a fully committed performance every moment you're on stage.

Never Make Fun of Someone's Laugh

This is an unwritten cardinal rule. When you make fun of someone's laugh, not only will that person stop laughing, but the rest of the audience will too because they don't want you to make fun of them. A person develops a loud or unusual laugh to get attention, so he or she often becomes the lead laugher for a crowd. If you squelch that person, you're likely to stifle the entire audience. You're on stage to make people laugh, so let them laugh.

The one exception is when the person's laugh overtakes your show. This is almost a form of inadvertent heckling. Here again, unfortunately, trying to shut this person up will often shut the crowd up as well. The only trick I've discovered for dealing with these laughers is to give them more attention than they really want until they laugh themselves out. I've gone so far as to keep encouraging a person to laugh until it's no longer fun because it's not interrupting the show. Then again, there are times when all you can do is work around an annoying laugh. Whatever the situation, never put someone down for their laugh.

Treat the Audience as a Group of Individuals

This is one of the best pieces of advice I can give you. If you don't relate to the audience as individuals, they'll feel you don't care about them. Take the time to make eye contact with several people. Tailor a joke to fit a specific person. Talk directly to different people as you share your material. After all, the audience is made up of individuals. They want to feel special too. Treat them this way, and they'll reciprocate in kind.

What to Do When the Audience Is Laughing

Knowing what to do when the audience is laughing is very important because if you do the wrong thing, they'll stop. Having to discuss this always amuses me. People who want to be funny spend a great deal of time writing jokes and rehearsing, and they take an enormous risk getting on stage. Then, when they get a laugh, they ignore it and keep talking.

SECRET #12:

WHEN THE AUDIENCE IS LAUGHING—SHUT UP.

Do you know how to train a flea? You put it in a jar, put some wax paper over the top, and poke holes in it so it can breath. The flea will try to jump out of the jar, but it'll smack into the wax paper. After several attempts, it will learn that it can only jump so high. Once this is accomplished, you can take the wax paper off and the flea will never jump out of the jar because it's been trained to stop.

Do you know how to train an audience to stop laughing? Same principle. I've watched comics train audiences to stop laughing simply by interrupting their laughter. (Read about writing past the *reveal* in Chapter 4.) When an audience begins to laugh and the comic talks into their laughter, they'll stop to hear what he's saying. If this happens often enough, the audience, like the trained flea, learns to pull up short. It's essential to allow the audience to laugh. Of course, if you make your relationship with the audience the most important thing, you'll be connected and know when to let them laugh. Following are some suggestions for what to do when the audience is laughing.

Freeze

Just stand still, become suspended in time until the laughter starts to taper off. This is very effective for short laughs. But freezing quickly becomes artificial, and difficult to hold during a very long laugh.

Remain Active and in the Same State of Mind You Were in When the Laugh Began

If you keep the state of mind you had when you told the joke, the audience will laugh, then when the laughter subsides, you'll be able to pick up right where you left off. This is not a freeze. For instance, if you were ranting and raving and pacing while you said the last joke, when they laugh, continue pacing with the same agitated intensity but without speaking. When they stop laughing, you'll have maintained the energy level so you can jump right back into ranting and raving.

Allow the Laughter to Affect You

The impact of the laughter on you emotionally will determine your interpretation and possibly prompt you to improvise what you say or do next. If you allow this feedback to lead you creatively, the show will reinvent itself. For the audience, there's a sense of danger in this kind of performing. There's a different spirit to a performance when you don't know what you're going to say next because the audience knows the show is based on their response. For instance, if you say a joke like:

I was involved in a love affair for two years—unassisted.

And someone laughs really loud, you can say something like:

You had one of those affairs, too.

Or continue to joke about your personal problem, like:

I guess this makes me a self-made man.

When the audience laughs at your problem, you can let that affect you, become a bit insulted, and fire back:

Thank you for laughing at my pain.

Think About What You're Going to Talk About Next

As long as you don't give any indication that you're going to speak, thinking about what you're going to say next is an extremely effective thing to do while the audience is laughing. Now, when I say *thinking* I mean seeing the picture of what you're going to talk about. If you've rehearsed the experiences, it'll be easy to remember them. These pictures, sounds, and feelings affect you emotionally and physically, and along with how the audience's laughter impacts you, this will determine what and how you'll say next. When they stop laughing, you may very well respond differently than you'd expected.

About Club Employees

If you want smooth-running shows you'll need to get along with the other people who work in the same environment. These people have a direct impact on the quality of your performances. They can help or hinder you, so you definitely want them on your side.

M.C.s

First of all, let me be clear. Here I'm discussing M.C.s at open-mike nights, not pros working on the circuit. Amateur M.C.s are often so inexperienced they can make an already difficult and scary job more difficult and scary. Officially, their job is to introduce the performers. But believe me, they have a great deal to do with the pace and mood of the show. A good or bad M.C. can make or break a show. And from my own and my students' experiences, most M.C.s at open-mikes are horrendous. They'll often trash anyone to get their laugh. On the flip side, being an M.C. is one of the most thankless jobs in comedy. If you're good at it, no one notices or says anything. If you're terrible at it, everyone will bad-mouth you. Nonetheless, M.C. is an invaluable position.

THE M.C. MAY BE IN CHARGE OF WHO GOES ON STAGE.

If you piss off the M.C. and he's the one who makes the lineup, you won't be on it. Some people need to have control and power, and then they wield it like Barney Fife. But no matter how much of an idiot they are, they've gotten themselves into a position of power. You'll want to be on the good side of these people.

DEVELOP A PERSONAL RELATIONSHIP.

When getting off stage, you could get complimented or trashed. Get to know the M.C. personally, so your chances of getting trashed are lessened. M.C.s can be cruel. Here's what I mean: I was watching an open-mike and the first-time comic was horrible. As if bombing wasn't enough, the M.C. came on stage and said:

You know how they pay some farmers not to grow crops . . .

It got a really good laugh, but it crushed the beginning comic. The M.C. is doing what he thinks is funny, but they're usually beginners too, so get used to them being inappropriate. If you can't stand the heat, don't join the fire department.

HAVE AN INTRODUCTION.

The M.C. may or may not read your intro, but if he does you have a better chance of getting on stage with some dignity. If you don't bring an intro, there's a better chance you'll get trashed.

BECOME AN M.C.

Getting into this position will help you get stage time. If you're a really good M.C. and you can make the audience laugh between comics, the audience will stay for the entire show to enjoy you. Then the club owner will want you to come back, not because you're so funny but because the audience stayed and drank more. The club owner is running a business, not an establishment for artists to experiment. If you become an M.C. you're the one with the power and control. Use it wisely because some comic you treat unfairly this year may be next year's sitcom producer. Being a really good M.C. is a valuable skill and it can help put you in a position to get stage experience.

Waitpersons

They have a very hard job to do in the first place. If you have ever been a cocktail waitperson, and I have, there's a great deal of pressure to get everyone served quickly, collect all the money at the last minute, and remain nice. Wanting them to be considerate of your show is an afterthought, and therefore a courtesy.

AGAIN, DEVELOP A PERSONAL RELATIONSHIP.

Waitpersons can have a negative influence on your show in many ways. They know the boss is more interested in serving drinks than in having a great show. They can serve at the right time or the wrong time. They can take orders in a whisper or a loud tone. When serving or taking orders, they can stand upright or squat down. If they like you, they'll do their best to be polite. If they don't like you, they can mess with your entire show just by the way they do their job.

DON'T DATE THE CLUB WAITPERSONS.

Develop a personal relationship but not too personal. In-club dating creates so many complications. It's not my job here to lay them all out, but if a dating situation becomes hurtful the club owner won't invite you back. That's bad for your business. After all, you're self-employed. Some clubs even have an official policy against the talent and the employees dating. Your best bet is to make your own rule not to date the waitpersons, or any club employee for that matter.

ENCOURAGE THE AUDIENCE TO TIP THE WAITPERSONS.

They usually work for minimum wage, so they make their real money from tips. If you're the voice that helps them make more tips, they'll be on your side. And if they're looking out for you just because they're nice people, encourage the audience to tip just because you can.

Bartenders

Bartenders are an interesting breed. They wield a fair amount of influence in a club because they interact with almost everyone. Some people have very little power in the world, so if they feel they can rationalize using it, they will to the hilt. It's much better to have these people as friends who enjoy laughing at you than as comedy terrorists making hit-and-run attacks on your shows.

AS ALWAYS, DEVELOP A PERSONAL RELATIONSHIP.
You may get tired of having me repeat this, but this is one of the most important auxiliary skills you can learn. If the bartender likes you, he or she will be considerate of your show. For instance, the bartender is in charge of the noisy machines like the register and blender. They can make those loud blender drinks or ring up the register just as you get to your punch, or they can wait a few seconds. They can yell drink orders or talk in a low tone. Also, they're responsible for the bar; they can allow extra complimentary drinks or charge you above your allotment.

TIP THE BARTENDER.
I've also been a bartender, and it's a very tough job. Like the wait staff, they want to be appreciated for what they do. If a bartender gives you a comp drink, put a buck or two in the tip bowl on the counter. A bartender who likes you will make your stay in the club and your show a much more pleasant experience.

Always Do Your Best

Give each performance your very best and take the responsibility for its success or failure. If you hold back you can't possibly get a truthful reading of how you're doing. For instance, if you're trying out a new joke and you only give it a half-hearted attempt, you're not giving it a fair shot. Fellow comedian Argus Hamilton once told me, "Do your new material on Saturday night. That way if it fails, it fails big, but if it succeeds, it succeeds big. Then you'll know if you want to keep it in your show or not."

Also, doing a half-assed job is the greatest excuse. If you weren't really trying, you won't have to deal with the truth about your show.

Without full commitment, you're just setting yourself up for failure. Commit and set yourself up to win.

Nothing will ever replace stage experience for teaching you what you need to know about being a comedian. So get out there and make 'em laugh, while you laugh all the way to the bank.

11

Fearless Performing

As with any art form, stand-up comedy will place you in a position of coming to grips with your own personal demons. Not only will you go through this struggle publicly, but you're also required to do it with a sense of humor. Fortunately, this chapter gives you the comedic tools you need for overcoming stage fright, handling hecklers, defusing a bomb, and keeping your memory remembering so you can approach any audience fearlessly.

Overcoming Stage Fright

I'm always amused by the term *stage fright* because it's so inaccurate. You aren't afraid of the stage, it's just a bunch of wood and concrete. What you're really afraid of is not living up to your own expectations or someone else's expectations while on stage. Actually, you rarely feel fear about what's happening in the present. Stage fright is really the result of imagining terrible things that might happen to you in the future.

Since you've accepted the comedy call to adventure, you might as well understand from the get-go that you'll be facing a fair amount of the *unknown*. It's called learning. It might help if you think of this as entering a strange, dark room. When you first open the door and step into the dark, it's very scary. So you shut the door and go away. But if you really want to know what's in that room, you'll come back, open the door, and step further into the dark. It's still scary, but not as much as the first time. If you're willing to take a workshop on stand-up comedy, a teacher can help by turning on the lights. Now you can survey the lit room and investigate the odd assortment of things you don't know how to use. The more you revisit the room, the quicker you'll learn that all of those unknown things are really just toys. And the more you play with them, the more fun you'll have, until they're no longer in the realm of the unknown, but have become your everyday playthings. Then a teacher like me comes along and opens another door.

Interestingly, there are two areas of performing where we feel fear. There's the preshow jitters and the feeling of fear while on stage. Following are some tips for overcoming both types of stage fright.

Preshow Jitters

When you take responsibility for your feelings you become empowered because you're in a position to do something about them, rather than just being a victim of them. In this section, you'll learn some ideas for turning your preshow jitters into an ally.

PUT IT IN PERSPECTIVE

You're one of five billion people on a little blue rock in the midst of a tiny solar system on the edge of the Milky Way Galaxy, in an obscure corner of the universe, and you have this little fear about getting on stage. Your problems are insignificant when you put them on a scale relative to the rest of the universe.

Also, you are one of the blessed because you have the luxury of going to a comedy club. There are people living in the middle of a war zone, their entire families have been killed, they have no food, and they fear that each moment may be their last. Your fear of getting on stage and facing a group of strangers pales by comparison.

I'm not suggesting that your feeling of fear isn't real or important. It is. But when you contrast it with what others must endure just to stay alive, having the opportunity to make people laugh puts you into some pretty privileged company. Enjoy it. And keep it in perspective.

REFRAME YOUR FEAR AS READINESS

Sometimes the way you think about something is what creates the problem. What if you've mistaken your feeling of fear for the feeling of readiness? To illustrate this point, the following is a story first told to me by my therapists, Phil and Norma Barretta:

> Before people were people, we were uncivilized prehumans. When danger was present, our unconscious minds would give us a shot of adrenalin to help us be more alert, quicker, stronger, ready to cope with an extraordinary situation. If there was a saber-toothed tiger

coming, we would get a shot of adrenalin preparing us for "fight or flight." We would either attack in order to make it our dinner or run away to avoid becoming its dinner. We accepted this shot of adrenalin as a gift to make us ready for an extraordinary situation.

Today when there's an extraordinary situation, we still get a shot of adrenalin. But now our conscious minds say, "Civilized people shouldn't feel fear." So we repress the feeling the adrenalin gives us. This confuses the unconscious mind, so it gives us another shot of adrenalin. We think we're feeling fear and since we fear the feeling of fear, we repress it yet again. This continues until we're so full of adrenalin that we begin shaking, which only confirms that feeling fear is bad.

If you're the intelligent being you think you are, accept the shot of adrenalin and thank your unconscious mind for the gift. Then it will determine that it's fulfilled its function of making you more alert, quicker, stronger, *ready* to cope with the extraordinary situation of getting on stage.

BE HONEST

You'll hear this piece of advice over and over again. Be blatantly honest in all matters. If you're scared, tell the audience you're scared. If you have to pee, tell the audience you have to pee. For many people it's not okay to have these feelings, so they try covering them up. The audience knows when you're afraid, so you might as well admit it. Then you won't spend the time or energy trying to hide it.

It *is* okay to have these feelings. You're doing something extraordinary, and your unconscious mind has just given you a shot of adrenalin to prepare you to be at your absolute best. And many times when you acknowledge and openly express your feelings, something miraculous happens. They dissolve.

CREATE A WARM-UP RITUAL

Briefly, find some sort of ritual that will keep your mind in the present by physically, psychologically, and creatively warming up. If you occupy your mind and body, you won't give yourself the space to imagine a terrifying result.

FEEL THE FEELINGS AND DO IT ANYWAY

Just before going onstage, I would always think, "Why am I doing this to myself?" The answer, of course, is that the benefits outweighed the momentary discomfort. When you have these feelings, acknowledge them, make it okay to feel them. Just don't let it stop you from doing what you want to do. As previously mentioned, what you're feeling is a shot of adrenalin. Feel it. Get to know it. As Robert Dilts, an NLP associate, says: "You don't want to get rid of the butterflies. What you want is for them to fly in formation."

STAY SOBER

Some people mistakenly believe the solution to their feeling of fear is by drinking some liquid confidence or smoking their cares away. Nothing could be further from the truth. Yeah, it might work once or twice, but very quickly it becomes a much larger problem than the feeling they're trying to mask.

The feeling you get before performing may never dissipate. Just because you guzzle booze or use dope to numb yourself to the feeling doesn't mean it's not there. It is. And when you ignore it, like any other signal, it'll get stronger and stronger. Which means you'll have to drink more or do more drugs to suppress it. This is not only stupid, but you might as well check in to the Betty Ford Clinic now. Stay sober and learn to manage your stage fright.

On Stage Fear

Most of the time, once you get on stage and start performing, your stage fright will simply disappear. But if it doesn't, there are several things you can do to overcome it.

SET SELF-CRITICISM ASIDE

What you're doing is already scary enough without your internal critic coming in and scolding you for not being perfect. Accept it, you're not perfect. You've just entered that strange, dark room. Give yourself some time to get to know what's in there. By dwelling on your shortcomings you can quickly talk yourself into immobilizing fear. Right now what you need is some support and suggestions in order to improve.

As I mentioned earlier, fear is a product of imagining some horrific future, especially one where your critic points out all the places where you could mess up. When you set your self-criticism aside, you'll be able to concentrate on the task at hand, which is relating your funny ideas to an audience.

STAY EMOTIONALLY ASSOCIATED WITH THE EXPERIENCES OF THE MATERIAL

Your conscious mind can only feel or express one thing at a time. It may appear that you're feeling many things, but they're actually one at a time in rapid succession. Getting past your fear has to do with where you're placing your attention. You can either focus on feeling fear or you can become involved in responding to the experiences within your jokes. When you're emotionally associated with the experiences of your material you'll stop focusing on the feelings *about* your performance and get lost in expressing the feelings *of* your performance.

Your stage fright may never go away, but if you employ one or all of these methods it will become manageable. The time to start worrying is when you stop getting that shot of adrenalin that makes you more alert, quicker, stronger, ready to cope with the extraordinary situation of getting on stage and making people laugh. What you want to achieve is for your stage fright to become an acceptable signal of encouragement.

Coping with Going Blank

Going blank is the second most common fear of fledgling comedians. From a teacher's perspective, I believe the sooner you go blank on stage the better. You'll handle it and survive. Once you realize that it's no big deal, you can not only cope with going blank, but you'll turn it into something funny.

Leave the Critic Off Stage

The presence of the Critic is one of the main reasons people go blank on stage. Self-criticism requires self-evaluation, so you focus your attention on yourself. As a result, you have no attention left for remembering, a condition described as *going blank*. Of course you aren't really blank. All kinds of things are going on in your head, and all of them are obstacles to remembering. The remedy for this dilemma is to separate your Critic and Creator when you rehearse.

Rehearse in the Same State in Which You Wish to Perform

Some people erroneously believe that they can run their show through their head and then be able to get on stage and do the show from their imagination. Actually, it only works if you just want to get on stage and just run your show through your head. But most audiences actually want to hear your show.

If you want to perform out loud, you must rehearse out loud. If you want to be emotionally associated, you must rehearse emotionally associated. If you want to play a character, you must rehearse playing the character. You must rehearse it as you wish to perform it or else you won't remember it.

Remain Playful

This is my advice for anything that goes wrong. If you're having fun, especially at troubled moments, the audience will stay with you. The worst part for the audience is feeling bad for you. They won't mind if you make a mistake or can't remember, as long as you're having fun. And when you're playful your sense of humor has a better chance of kicking in so you can turn the situation into something funny.

One of my female students would only rehearse by thinking about her show, no matter how often I warned her that she wouldn't be able to remember it under the stress of being on stage. Predictably, when she did her nightclub showcase she went completely blank. Fortunately for her, "remain playful" was one piece of advice she'd taken to heart. She kept making fun of the fact that she couldn't remember and getting consistent laughs. To support her I yelled out the subject of one her strongest bits. She retorted,

> Oh thanks, Greg, now I have to stay up here and actually do my show.

This got a big laugh. She struggled through her show with dignity by remaining playful. Afterward, she conceded that maybe she should have rehearsed out loud after all.

Be Honest

The audience won't mind if you forget for a moment, but they'll want to know what's going on. Don't try to hide it. Admit it outright. Just say,

> I've just forgotten everything I've ever known.

The audience will probably empathize with your fear of going blank and laugh. If you try to hide it, your energy and attention will be focused on concealing it or wondering whether they've noticed. Often, if you just admit that you've forgotten, your memory will miraculously come back.

Take a Breath

The stress of performing can make you physically tense. If you take a moment to breathe deeply, you'll realize you're just fine. My lady, Gayla Johnson, not only tried this, but feeling that the whole audience was also uptight, she asked them to take a deep breath with her. They did and exhaled with a laugh.

Check Your Show List

The code words will remind you of where you are in your show. You can pick it up where you forgot, or dump the whole bit and try something else.

Try Riffing

Riffing is talking with the audience, asking them questions . . .

> Hi, what's your name? What do you do for a living?

. . . and making jokes out of their answers. An extremely useful tool, it takes the attention off yourself and helps you reestablish a relationship with the audience. It helps to practice it.

Riffing can be a scary thing to do, but it's better than standing there with your thumb up your butt.

Dealing with Bombing

Bombing is the number one fear associated with doing stand-up comedy. When your show isn't getting any laughs, life stops being a movie and you're thrust into the awareness that you're really here in front of people, a flush of tingly heat spreads over your face, all you can hear is a deafening roar of silence, and then your internal self-talk starts screaming, "Why am I doing this to myself!" Your mouth feels as if it's stuffed with cotton, your heart is thumping in your chest, and beads of perspiration snake down your face. You're experiencing what comedians refer to as *flop sweat*.

If this description is enough to scare you away from wanting to be a comic, quit now because bombing is an inevitable aspect of being a funny person. Accept it and prepare yourself to handle it resourcefully.

In one of my classes, a student had been bombing for five minutes straight when I finally asked, "Have you noticed that no one has laughed in the last five minutes?" "Yes," he replied, "but I didn't want it to affect me." But you should want it to affect you. It'll feel so bad, you'll want to do something about it.

SECRET #13:
IF WHAT YOU'RE DOING ISN'T WORKING—DO ANYTHING ELSE.

Anything else? Yes. Anything else. You must have the flexibility to shift and change because anything different is better than repeating what isn't working. The new thing you choose may not work either, but at least now you know two things to avoid.

Bombing isn't just the suffering part of being a comic. It's the learning part. If you never bomb, you'll never learn. From bombing you usually learn what doesn't work, which is just as important as knowing what does.

With comedy, as with anything you learn, you'll be ineffective some of the time. It's just that in comedy, your faltering is so damn public. But you have a choice about how you respond to "eating the big one." You can frame it as *failure* or *feedback*. If you choose to view bombing as failure, you're bound for a spot among the multitudes who've tried stand-up a couple of times, bombed, felt like a loser, and quit. But if you want to do this for a living, you'll find it very helpful to reframe bombing as useful feedback.

In comedy you get clear and instant feedback. The audience either laughs or doesn't laugh. To improve your show, you must take responsibility for how it went, honestly face shortcomings, and correct them.

This chapter is full of skills, principles, and techniques to guide you in creating a successful show. But remember, you will bomb, so be prepared. Here are some helpful hints for dealing with bombing.

Continue to Commit

Remember, whatever state you're in, the audience is in. If you give up on your show, they will too. If being funny isn't worth your total commitment, get out. I mean this. Sure, you're going to have some really bad nights. So what? If you really want to be a comedian, then you'd better be willing to give it your all every time you get on stage. There are a butt-load of comedians who give their very best night after night, and you simply won't be able to compete with them.

Whenever you pull back, you just make matters worse because you've stopped doing your best. But if you stay committed, there's always a chance that you can turn the show around. I've done it, and I've seen it done hundreds of times. But if you dog out on your own show, you have nobody to blame but yourself. If you don't care enough to stay committed to your own show, neither will anyone else.

Keep Your Sense of Humor

To demonstrate what I really mean by this, let me start by making a distinction between a *sense of funny* and a *sense of humor*. A sense of funny is knowing what makes *other people* laugh. A sense of humor is what makes *you* laugh. If your sense of funny is off on a particular night, it helps to have a sense of humor about it. In other words, if you think it's funny that you suck, the audience will enjoy your ability to laugh at yourself. Then the least that can happen is that you'll have a great time bombing.

The biggest problem with not getting laughs isn't the lack of laughter; it's the horrid state of mind that it creates. The worse you feel about how badly things are going, the worse the audience will feel. They'll want you to get off stage, not because your jokes aren't getting laughs but because they feel so bad for you. But if it's okay with you that the show isn't funny, and you're even willing to make fun of the fact, the audience will go along. If you have a sense of humor about bombing, when you leave the stage the audience might say something like, "He wasn't very funny, but I sure enjoyed watching him try." If you keep your sense of humor, the audience will almost always pull for you.

156

One more note—I believe that the sense of humor evolved in humans as a means of dealing with the painful things. Bombing certainly fits in this category, and your sense of humor should automatically kick in to deal with it. It may be embarrassing, but it's even worse to crash and burn without a sense of humor. When you bomb with a sense of humor, at least you'll leave the stage with your dignity.

Be Honest

This is the most important thing you need to do when your show is flopping. The audience needs to know *that you know* you're bombing. The best way to let them know this is by mentioning it. As long as you're willing to honestly acknowledge the truth about what's happening, *the audience will always trust you.*

When a comic ignores the fact that he isn't getting any laughs, the audience wonders, "Gee, has he noticed that he isn't funny?" If it goes on for too long, they stop trusting the comic because it's clear that he hasn't noticed or doesn't care. Eventually, the audience stops listening, and when that happens, you can hear the suction from the whirlpool pulling you under.

Admit that your jokes aren't getting laughs. It's not a crime. You have nothing to apologize for. You're taking a huge risk just by getting on stage, and that's something to be proud of even if you fail. But those who haven't tried it don't know this, so make it okay by playfully talking about it.

Don't make excuses, either. You took the risk, you take the consequences. The audience expects you to handle it. Excuses just make you look like a cheese weenie who cops out when things don't go your way. Just do your best to rectify the situation and keep searching for their funny bone.

When you're brutally honest about the shortcomings of your show, an amazing thing usually happens—the audience laughs. They aren't used to someone being so straightforward about a show that's faltering, and it'll shatter their assumption. In comedy, honesty is the best policy.

Use a Saver

A *saver* is a line that's not regularly in your show but kept in the back of your mind for emergency situations. And bombing is an emergency situation. When you're drowning, a saver can help you keep afloat.

Here are a few:

That joke was much funnier when I wrote it.

Whoever said "Silence is golden" was never a stand-up comic.

My favorite saver was written by my student Kevin Comstock:

I'm doing a thing I call *stealth comedy*. It's where either the jokes sneak up on you or it appears that there are no jokes at all.

Ask for Suggestions

If things are consistently bad, talk to the audience about it. Be prepared for them to give you advice, like "Get off the stage." or "Don't give up your day job." But if you can get past all that and get an answer from someone, you'll learn a valuable lesson about how you affect an audience.

When Michael Davis and I were doing street shows at Renaissance Faires in California, in the late 1970s, we did a bit in our show where, after Michael finished a really nice juggling trick, I'd come over to him with a mop on my shoulder, shake his hand, then turn to walk away so the mop would swing around and smack him in the face. This is an old clown gag we learned when we were working in Ringling Bros. and Barnum and Bailey Circus. We had gotten so good at it that the audience stopped laughing and began to gasp in horror at Michael taking such a hard hit in the face. (In reality, I was downstage a foot and the mop barely touched his face.) I didn't like this gasping response because I wanted a laugh. During one show, I asked the audience why they were gasping, and someone yelled, "You hit him too hard with that mop." I thanked the person, explained that I hadn't, and got back into our show. After the show, Michael and I talked about it, then rehearsed the mop-in-the-face gag until we could do it less realistically. We got our laugh back.

Talk to your audience. They're real people with opinions about what you're doing. If you're willing to hear it, you'll grow much faster than the comics who think the audience is stupid. This is not to say that you should heed everything you get from an audience, but it's better to have the information and not use it than not to have it at all.

Make Your Material More Personal to the Audience

One of the many mistakes that leads to bombing is saying your show *at* an audience. Relating to the audience as a group of individuals can really energize a show. Reword a joke to specify someone sitting in the second row. Convince the audience that the things you're talking about are absolutely real by speaking directly to someone. Sit down at someone's table, all the while doing your show. Sit on someone's lap. Relate a joke to one person, then tell that same joke to another person, and compare the response.

A personal show is a compelling show. The audience stays attentive because at any time you might chat with them. Even if you aren't bombing, this is the way I believe a show should be handled—as an interpersonal communication rather than a presentation.

Respond with More Emotional Intensity

To understand the reason for this piece of advice, remember that jokes are a *response*. When a show is falling flat, it is often because you're just saying the words of the jokes. Cranking up the emotional intensity will force you to respond to what you're talking about. At least this will energize the show and make it more interesting.

Deliver the Jokes at Different Speeds

If you think you've been going too fast, slow down. If you suspect you've been going too slow, speed up. If what you're doing isn't working—do something else.

Do Only Your Best Jokes

You know which of your jokes are great, which are good, and which are marginal. If you feel as if you're getting sucked down into that funnel of silence, stop trying to do a show with a story line and cut to the best of the best. Tell the audience what you're doing, and say, "Okay, I know this isn't going well, but what about this joke?" Skip around your show in an attempt to find the material that'll hit. Finding a cluster of jokes they'll laugh at might kick-start the rest of your show.

Try Riffing

Riffing when your show is bombing has a different function than riffing when you've gone blank. Here, you're doing "something else" in an effort to discover the audience's level. Riffing, even badly, is better than continuing to do material that isn't working. And when you're riffing, the audience knows you're taking a risk to make them laugh. Most of the time, they'll stay with you as long as you're giving it your best shot.

After the Show, Deal with It

When a show is over ask yourself, "Did I do the best I could?" If the answer is yes, then you've succeeded. You can't do better than your best. That doesn't mean that you should stop improving, but when you've done your best, feel good about it.

Go off by yourself, run over in your mind the things that went wrong, and how you can handle them more effectively next time. Since hindsight is 20/20, you're sure to come up with a slew of things you could have done. Keep them in the back of your mind for future reference. After all, where do you think the ideas in this section came from?

Once you've gone over your alternatives, you've done your job, so drop it. Don't waste energy browbeating yourself over what's done. Instead, use the time to plan and prepare your next show.

Crossing the Hurt Line

When someone or something appears to be *truly* hurt, the show turns into drama. That's the difference between comedy and drama. Comedy doesn't deal with the true consequences of hurtful things. Someone or something *can* be hurt, but not *really* hurt; more like cartoon hurt. Think of a time when you saw someone take a ridiculous fall and began to laugh; then when you realized they were hurt, you stopped laughing and went to help. An audience reacts the same way. If they feel someone or something is truly hurt, they won't laugh.

This goes for imaginary things as well. If you pretend to kick a dog as part of your joke, and the audience feels that the imaginary dog is hurt, they might groan or even boo you. Strange, isn't it?

It's also true about you. If you're bombing and appear to be hurt *by* not doing well, the audience will feel sorry for you. Then they'll want you to get off stage so the pain they feel for you will stop.

One other thought. The hurt line moves. One audience's hurt is another audience's hilarity. This is why you have to read your audience and interpret the material specifically for them. Certain audiences will buy into some really mean material, while others want things to stay nice and light. It's your job to feel this out and customize your show accordingly.

Handling Hecklers

Heckling is an audience disease. Being mercilessly heckled is the third most common fear associated with stand-up comedy. Just the prospect of a heckler deters some beginners from getting on stage because they don't know if they'll be able to cope with it. But, as with all things, the reality isn't nearly as frightening as our fantasy. When handling a heckler, your goal is to remain in charge of yourself and your show.

SECRET #14:

MOST HECKLERS THINK THEY'RE HELPING MAKE YOUR SHOW BETTER.

Most hecklers are misguided, not malicious. They like you and want to help, so they yell out comments they think make the show funnier. They're not familiar with concepts such as the flow of one joke to the next or the building of a rhythm throughout an entire show. Unbeknownst to them, their remarks can interrupt these invisible functions that only comics know about. All they understand is that they made a comment and got a laugh, then the comic came back and got an even bigger laugh. "Hey, we're a team."

Handling hecklers effectively is a skill that is only acquired through a great deal of stage experience. In the meantime, here are some helpful hints to stave off the scourge.

Ignore Comments

It may surprise you, but if you disregard their first couple of remarks, hecklers will usually get embarrassed and shut up, or their friends will punch on them to make them be quiet. This was the hardest lesson for me to learn. As a beginner, I was always of the mind that if there was a peep during my show, I'd tromp on it to get back the control. This almost always turned into a confrontation. But one time, I was tired so I ignored a heckler, and he didn't heckle me anymore. Once he realized that I wasn't going to enter into an exchange, he just gave up. It was so much easier, and the show went more smoothly because to deal with a heckler you have to stop your show, do what you have to do, then try to build the rhythm of the show again. If you ignore them, there's a better chance you can just keep going.

Remain Playful

No matter how nasty your comments, they still must be in the spirit of fun. If it appears that you're trying to *hurt* the heckler, the audience will turn against you because the hurt line has been crossed. Remember, whatever state you're in, the audience is in. If you become mean and vengeful, the audience will become mean and vengeful. The heckler may be messing up your show, but you can always make it worse by attacking without a sense of humor. The audience is there to laugh, not watch you seek personal retribution from some jerk. Once it stops being funny, you're not doing your job.

Make Sure They Deserve It

This is so important. The time to verbally cut down a heckler is when the audience is just as irritated with him as you are. If the audience doesn't perceive that he deserves it, they'll view you as an overly aggressive jerk.

Another Chippendale's story: One night I was doing a show and two very beautiful ladies were sitting about three feet to my right. They considered me to be an obstacle to them getting to see the male exotic dancers, a common audience attitude that I had to overcome as the opening act. These ladies were particularly nasty. They said personal things about me, just loud enough so only I could hear them. Things like, "God, he's got such bad skin. He's kind of ugly." "Get him off and bring out the real men." This was really tough for me, so I tore into them with several mean lines. They shut up. But, of course, so did the rest of the audience. Only I had heard the comments, so all the audience saw was my vicious attack on these two ladies for no apparent reason. I didn't even realize this until after the show when one of the waiters asked me why, out of the blue, I started yelling at those two ladies. It doesn't matter if they deserve it, only that the audience perceives that they deserve it. On the other hand, once the audience perceives that they deserve it, kick butt.

Avoid Taking Things Personally

There are people who go to comedy clubs who find their fun in messing with the comics. From my perspective these people are scum, but nonetheless, from time to time, you'll have an encounter with this sort of cretin. If a heckler can push your buttons, he'll control you and the show. I know it's difficult to avoid getting personally hooked because you care so much about doing your best. But a heckler who gets to you can put you at your worst.

Never Invite the Heckler on Stage

Guess why I know about this. When I was first beginning back in the mid-70s in San Francisco, I was working at a hole-in-the-wall club known as the Holy City Zoo. I was being heckled mercilessly when I lost my temper and said, "If you think you can do any better, then come up and try." This one did. He pushed me out of the way and proceeded to tell one really funny joke. The guy running the open-mike night came over, I thought to help me, but instead he told the heckler to get off stage, then turned on me and yelled, "There are tons of people who have signed up to get on this stage. You can't put anyone you want up here. Don't ever do that again. Now finish your show."

Does the word *mortified* seem appropriate here? I was so devastated that I didn't do stand-up for the next six months. Never invite a heckler on stage because, oddly enough, most people can tell one really funny joke. He'll get the laugh and you'll look like a jerk.

Use Heckler Lines

Heckler lines aren't as easy to use as you might think. Just because you have a series of great insults memorized doesn't mean that that's all there is to handling hecklers. It's a whole psychological game that you'll need to learn. Be prepared with a variety of comebacks to fit the different kinds of heckles. You can write them yourself or get them from insult joke books. For example:

Out of millions of sperm, you had to be the quickest.

Now you know why some animals eat their young.

Isn't it sad when cousins marry.

Jesus loves you, but everyone else thinks you're an asshole.

163

I'm sorry. I didn't mean to interrupt your heckling with my show.

Shut up.

Sometimes, the simpler the better. If you get two hecklers, there's the ever popular:

Oh great. Stereo assholes.

Easy on the Women

You can't blast women as hard as you can men, no matter how much they deserve it. You could call this sexism, and maybe it is, but it's also a comedy reality. Everyone has a primordial instinct to protect women. Even women comics can't hit women as hard as they can men. Of course, female hecklers are far less common than male. To deal with female hecklers, you must walk a fine line. If you hit them with too harsh a line, the audience will turn on you. Then again, if you're not forceful enough, they'll continue heckling and ruin your show.

Here are a few examples:

It's all right, I remember the first time I drank a beer.

Is this cheaper for you than seeing a psychiatrist?

The last time you heckled me, didn't you wear that same dress?

Please. Shut up.

The best idea I've heard recently comes from my friend and comic juggler, Frank Olivier. He says, "Attack the man she's with and she'll shut up." Here's one of Frank's lines:

And look at the guy she's with. I guess I'd look like that too if each morning I woke up with a woman like that.

Challenge Them to Continue to Make More Remarks

This turns the tables so you can berate them for not coming up with clever comments. If they do hit a good one, then prod them to say more. They'll quickly run out of steam. The aim is to embarrass them into submission by goading them on. Here's a paraphrase of one of my sessions following a comment from a male heckler:

That was very funny. Any more? Come on, you Don Rickles wan-na-be. Have at it. Come on. You've gotta have a couple more.

The heckler shot back:

You're not as clever as you think you are.

He was clearly flailing, so I nailed him with:

Another scathing comment from our literary wizard. That sucked. Come on Dale Carnegie, speak up. Oh, now that I give you the chance to talk you won't. Come on, let everyone know why you need attention during someone else's show. I don't go to where you work and take away your shovel.

Of course, this must be done with a sense of play, but mean-spirited play because you want the heckler to know he's not welcome to talk out loud during your show. I've found this effective in several shows. Then again, I've also really pissed off some people. But hey, if they take the risk, they also have to accept the consequences.

Sincerely Ask Them to Stop

I know this seems too simple to be true, but it really works. Since most hecklers think they're helping your show, sometimes just nicely asking them to stop can be enough. I've even gone so far as to admit that I'm not as good as they are and to please give me a chance. It's so disarming to have the performer pleasantly request that you not comment, that most people will agree. After all, the goal is to be able to do your show without heckler interruptions. Try sincerity. It works. Really. But if it doesn't—trash the bastards.

Survive the Drunks and the Drugged

Every so often, you'll encounter a heckler that's oblivious to the fact that he or she is acting like an ass and ruining your show. Someone like this just won't shut up, no matter what you do. Back at Chippendale's one night, there was a woman drunk and drugged into another dimension. As soon as I entered she screamed in a three-packs-of-cig-arettes-a-day, phlegm-filled, raspy voice: "Taaaaake it ooooff."

I was used to the women saying "Take it off" because it's the phrase they yell at the male strippers. I went with my standard comeback:

Sorry. Mine's not detachable.

This got a good laugh. But that night this lady didn't hear me. She didn't hear anybody. She just kept screaming, "Taaaaake it ooooff." I ignored the next few, but she was on a program of repeating it about every thirty seconds, so ignoring her didn't work. I tried a heckler line:

I bet guys like you for your personality.

The audience was with me, so they hooted and applauded. But the drunk lady persisted every thirty seconds or so. After about the seventh or eighth time, I picked up her cue of taking a huge breath before screaming. So I'd pause, let her scream "Taaaaake it ooooff," and continue my joke. The audience could see I was maneuvering around her.

I even ad-libbed one joke. Just about the time I figured she'd scream, I said:

Later, the male exotic dancers are going to come out here and you're going to want to yell—"

Right on cue, she screamed; "Taaaaake it ooooff."

It got a huge laugh. But it was getting increasingly difficult to do my show because I only had so many minutes on stage and she was using them up. I decided to try one more ploy. Sincerity. I went to her, knelt down, covered my mike so the audience couldn't hear, looked her and her friends in the eyes and said, "Please, it's been fun, but I really want to be able to do my show. I'd really appreciate it if you'd stop yelling. Please." Seemingly affected by my request, the drunk lady replied, "Taaaaake it ooooff."

Sometimes there isn't a solution. She was so drunk that communication of any kind was futile. Just do your best to entertain the people who are with you. It's not personal, the messed up person has a problem, not you. Chalk it up as to one show a heckler screwed up.

Ignore the Section with the Heckler

This tip came to me by way of the comedian Michael Colyar, who says to overtly ignore the heckler's section of the audience. Give all the attention to the area of the crowd that's being respectful and attentive. This creates a kind of rivalry for the comic's attention. Since the ignored section wants the comic's attention back, they'll turn on the heckler and get him to shut up. It's a smarter choice to get the audience to do the work for you.

After the Show

Take the time to review what you did right and think of some ways you can handle it more effectively next time. If you take the time to evaluate and consider new options, you'll be more prepared the next time you get a heckler.

If after the show a heckler comes up to you, don't get mad or put them down because this will only help them rationalize that you deserved to be heckled. Then again, don't let them off the hook by being too nice about it either. Instead, explain to them that they made your job harder. When I was working the Comedy Store in Westwood, California, a heckler commented through my entire show. I dealt with it well and got several laughs with my comebacks. After the show, the heckler came over to buy me a beer. I declined. He got indignant and said, "What are you upset about? I helped you get a lot of laughs." I admitted that that was true, then explained that his heckle interrupted me during the setup of a seventeen-joke routine. Because I had to stop to deal with his comments, my stage time had dwindled to the point to where I had to cut the entire routine. He created a situation where I got two laughs but had to sacrifice seventeen. That's fifteen laughs I lost. He began to apologize. I still didn't accept his beer, gathered my things, and went home with the feeling that maybe there was one less heckler in the world.

Only a great deal of stage time will teach you how to cope with going blank, deal with bombing, and handle hecklers, but heeding this advice will place you far ahead of those who just lash out at an audience when things are going wrong. It important to understand there's always a solution that can get a laugh.

12

Getting Experience

Getting stage time is the most important factor in the education of an aspiring comic. I can teach you many comedy techniques, but the only thing that will teach you to be funny is performing in front of people. Many beginners make the mistake of waiting for the "right time" to try stand-up comedy. This is—how can I put it delicately—a big load of crap. There is no right time, there's only right *now*.

In my opinion, there's only one force strong enough to drive you to become a professional funny person: an intense love for making people laugh. They can't pay you enough money to go through what you'll need to go through to learn to be a comic. For starters, there's the fact that most of what you'll learn about being funny will be things that *don't work*. The only way to learn what *does* work is through trial and error. So when you're a beginner at stand-up comedy, you're going to fail. More than once. This is not a comforting thought, but you might as well get used to it. Remember, if something's worth doing, it's worth doing badly. If you find this prospect discouraging, quit now and save yourself a lot of turmoil.

SECRET #15:
PERFORM ANYWHERE YOU CAN GET IN FRONT OF PEOPLE.

Anywhere? Yes. Anywhere. You'll be surprised at some of the places I'm going to suggest. And don't expect to be paid. To develop as a funny person, you need experience and time to work on your material. Once you have a solid 20- to 25-minute show with which you can be consistently funny night after night in club after club, you can begin searching for work. Until then, they are many places to get experience.

Open-Mikes

These are nightclubs, restaurants, coffee houses, and so on, that let anyone get up and take a shot at doing three to six minutes of stand-up comedy. If you can be funny at an open-mike, you can probably be funny anywhere. However, there are a few things you need to know.

Don't Expect to Be Treated Fairly

These places seldom provide pleasant experiences. Most often, you'll be going onstage very early, before anyone's come in, or very late, when everyone's left. If you're lucky enough to get an audience at all, it'll probably consist of other comics waiting to go on or three drunks eating chili and farting. But keep the faith. Remember, it's always darkest just before it gets pitch black.

Sign-Ups Are Usually in Advance

You usually have to sign up for open-mike nights earlier in the day or sometimes a week or more in advance. This can be time-consuming, but make the commitment anyway.

You'll Get Bumped by the Regulars

There will be times when the club regulars will bump you to a later spot or knock you off the roster altogether. I know it's frustrating, but until you have more seniority, expect to be the low person on the comedy totem pole. Your time will come.

Heed the Signal to Get Off-Stage

Many clubs have some kind of a light or signal to let you know it's time to get off-stage. Heed it well. If you go more than thirty seconds over, they'll become more forceful about getting you off. Worse yet, they may ask you not to come back.

Showcase Clubs' Unpaid Spots

Showcase clubs present a string of ten or more comics in an evening, opposed to a traditional club, which has a lineup consisting of only three comics—an opener, middle, and headliner. Getting a regular spot at a showcase club will accelerate your growth as a comedian because you'll have a consistent place to work out. These are hard to come by, but there are some tips that should help you.

Target a Club and Hang Out There as Often as Possible

The more you're around, the more you schmooze with the right people, the better your chances of getting stage time. Paying your dues in comedy can be an unstated test of endurance. If you stick it out through all the crap—and there will be more than a shovelful—everyone will know you're serious about a career in comedy.

Do Clean Material

This is a recurring theme in this chapter for several reasons. If all of your laughs come from the shock value of foul language, you're not writing jokes. You're just shattering the assumptions of social propriety. Also, you can never use blue material on commercial television, and network TV is probably where your first national break will come from. Maybe you're saying, "But Eddie Murphy does blue stuff and he's a star." True, but his break came from *Saturday Night Live* and from movies where he had to rely as much on his acting ability as his comedy. Now that he's a star, he can do what he pleases. Finally, club bookers are more inclined to put clean comedians on their stages. In fact, many absolutely insist on it.

Keep It on Time

Going over your allotted time is another mistake beginners make. This can create ill will toward you on the part of the club bookers and the other comedians on the bill because it makes the show end later.

Organize Your Own Show

Find a restaurant, bar, or dance club that has a P. A. system and a microphone and offer to put together a comedy night. Most owners of these establishments will cooperate if you convince them it will bring in more business at little or no cost to them. You may have to do all the organizing and even pay for advertising, but if you can pull it off you'll have a decent place to perform. If possible, pool your resources with other beginning comics and delegate some of the responsibilities.

Build a Little Stage

If the owner will let you, construct an elevated stage. It's psychologically helpful for a performer to be above the crowd. When you're on the same level or lower than your audience, trying to be funny can sometimes be a discouraging venture.

Make the Comics Bring the Audience

Many clubs are doing this now. The amount of time the comic gets to perform is determined by the number of butts he or she puts in the nightclub seats. No butts—no show.

My significant other, Gayla Johnson, and student Dave Reinitz, put together a show at a restaurant on the Universal City Walk here in Los Angeles. To ensure getting a good audience, they turned the show into a contest. The winner was to be determined by audience vote, so the comics were motivated to bring in as many people as they could. Every ten weeks all the winners were brought back for a semifinal, which had a cash prize donated by the restaurant. In 1995, the finals of their contest happened to coincide with the American Comedy Festival sponsored by Comic Relief, which was held at City Walk, and they were included as part of the festival. As of this writing the contest is still going on and everyone is pleased, especially Gayla and Dave, because they have a place to perform every week.

Toastmasters

Toastmasters is a national organization dedicated to public speaking. They have regular meetings at which members and guests make speeches. If you speak at a Toastmaster meeting, there's no reason why you can't use your comedy routine as your speech. Several of my students have won contests put on by this organization.

Charity and Civic Club Meetings

Many public service organizations have gatherings all the time, and some are open to including entertainment. They exist to support the community, so offering people a chance to entertain in public can be part of their agenda. When you get good at your craft, performances for these groups can become paying gigs. Be careful to do only very clean material.

Social Parties

If you can't wrangle a way to do some kind of a show, then make your conversation at social gatherings a vehicle for your material. Do your jokes without anyone knowing that you're practicing on them.

Back in the mid-70s, I was notorious for doing shows at parties. Whenever the room fell silent, I would break into some kind of comedy routine. Maybe it was partly that everyone was stoned out of their minds, but I would get big laughs. One year when I was broke at Christmas, I made the rounds of the homes of my friends and relatives and did a short show I'd created especially for the occasion as their present. Some thought it was great. Others considered me out of my comic mind. I was young—so both were okay with me.

In Parks or on the Streets

Don't scoff—I started at city parks in my hometown of Modesto, California, going from picnic table to picnic table. A few years later, I made good money doing a comedy–juggling act on Fisherman's Wharf in San Francisco.

A funny and talented African American comedian, Michael Colyar, began his career in Chicago doing what he called Guerilla Comedy. He'd go to State Street and do a show for people on their lunch breaks. He moved to Los Angeles to work year-round on the Venice Beach boardwalk because, he said, "In Chicago, they don't want to hear no jokes in the snow." He went on to win $100,000 on *Star Search*, half of which he graciously donated to the homeless. Since then, he's had many national television spots and appeared in more than a dozen movies. Seriously consider performing in any crowded public arena.

Dance Bars

Michael Colyar shared with me another of his original tactics for getting experience. In search of a different venue for his show, he went to a dance bar to check out the scene. Noticing that at a certain point people would get tired of dancing and leave, he persuaded the owner of the bar to let him do a fifteen-minute comedy show on the dance floor. The deal was that if the patrons of the club didn't like him, he'd never come back, but if they loved him the club owner would pay him $30. As it turned out, the people really did love Michael, and after his show they were rested and up for more dancing and drinking. The club owner, who was making more money, paid willingly. On the basis of this success, Michael convinced ten other dance clubs to let him do the same thing. Soon he was making $300 a week doing his comedy show in dance bars. Another triumph for Guerilla Comedy.

Never complain that there's nowhere to perform. Create a place. Every new option you try will add to your knowledge and style. Some experiences will be horrifying, some will be fun, some will be both—but that's not the point. The important thing is to accumulate as much time performing in public as you can. Remember, good judgment comes from experience; and experience comes from bad judgment.

But by far, the best piece of advice I can give you is:

JUST GET OUT THERE AND DO IT—NOW!

13

Making a Good Show Great

Polishing a show is a continual evolutionary loop of developing material, rehearsing, performing, and polishing, which leads back to developing material, rehearsing, performing, and so on. All professional comedians eventually devise some sort of method for sharpening up their shows, but there's no "right way" or "best way" to do this.

It's not really productive to work on improving your show until *after* you've performed it in front of an audience. Why? Because there's only so much that past experience and intuition can tell you about how an audience is going to respond to a joke or routine.

The following guidelines can help you create your own working style. They're derived from ideas I developed while teaching and observing working comedians, as well as standard comic knowledge. Here's a suggested method for polishing your show:

- Play back the show
- Rate the jokes
- Edit, rewrite, and rearrange
- Rehearse and perform again

These are just guidelines, *not* a rigid step-by-step procedure. So feel free to customize them by changing the order, skipping around, or adding your own touches. Also, keep in mind that polishing, as it's defined here, is an ongoing process designed to continually refine your show, not a fix-all you can run through just once.

Play Back the Show

Playing back your show is the best way to discover what works and what doesn't. It's a good idea to go all the way through the entire show first to get a general idea of where the highs and lows are. Then go back over it again, sentence by sentence, joke by joke, and routine by routine. Use the pause or stop button after every sentence or joke so you have time to gage each one; your evaluation will be more effective if you look at smaller chunks.

The audiotape recorder used to be the most popular means of recording a show, but with the advent of the palm-sized video recorder, videotaping has become more prevalent in clubs. Some clubs even have an inhouse camera and will videotape your show for a fee. If the price is reasonable, you should take advantage of this service. A videotape is an enormous advantage when polishing your show.

If you think you're going to remember what happened during your show, you're wrong. Usually, you'll recall very little of a show you've done, especially the ad-libs. And it's virtually impossible to remember details about the audience's response to every joke. Use some device to record your show so you can play it back.

Rate the Jokes

When you go over your show, have a list of your jokes on a sheet of paper or the computer screen with a space to write in a score for each one. As you play back each joke, rate it according to the laughs it gets. Give those that get the biggest laughs an A; the medium a B; and the worst a C. If a joke doesn't get a laugh, but a smile, give it a D. And if it receives silence, rate it an F.

Using this process, you'll eventually fill your entire show with A material. As you develop better material, you'll take out the Cs. In time, you'll even edit the B material. Finally, you'll have a show with nothing but As. Achieving this goal is no easy task, especially when you consider that most comics find that only about 10 percent of all the jokes they write make it permanently into their regular shows. And of those jokes, only about 10 percent or fewer qualify as As. Those numbers would suggest that something like one out of a hundred jokes you write will turn out to be an A. I don't say this to discourage you, but to make it clear how important it is to keep a regular writing schedule so that you're constantly coming up with new material. If you write just one A joke a week, you'll have fifty-two great jokes at the end of a year. That's about thirty minutes of new A material, or approximately four or five TV-length sets.

You can be sure that the top comedians on *Letterman, The Tonight Show,* or with their own cable special aren't doing any of their Bs or Cs. If you want to be one of them, you'll work toward doing the same.

Here are my ratings for the jokes I wrote for a post office routine. There are two grades for each joke because I rated two different performances to get a better reading. The first line is the introduction to my routine, so I didn't rate it.

How can I bring up the subject of the post office without sounding angry? I can't. So, here we go.

D-D First of all, the post office has the audacity to have the logo of an eagle streaking through the sky. Yeah, right. It should be something more like a slug taking a nap.

D-D It frustrates me because the post office is a monopoly. If it had to operate like a real business, it'd be about as successful as a steak house in India.

C-D Just the term *postal service* is an oxymoron.

C-C The other day, I was standing in line and I was checking out one of those mug shots of this particularly tough, nasty looking lowlife—it was the employee of the month.

F-F I'd been in line for about ten minutes and it's getting even longer, so I yelled, "The line is getting longer, can you *please* close one of the windows." They did.

C-B Maybe I'm being too tough on postal workers. After all, they are actually very efficient—with guns.

C-B Hey, their motto is "Neither snow, nor rain, nor gloom of night shall keep them from their *rounds.*"

B-C And the thing that gets me, I don't understand why so many postal workers kill other postal workers. You'd think they'd be killed by disgruntled customers.

A-A After hearing me trash the post office, a postal worker said to me, "You shouldn't insult postal workers." I said, "Why not?" He said, "Because we know where you live."

C-A I said, "Even if you did come after me, you'd show up at the wrong house."

D-C To change the subject a little bit, I asked him, "Why is it that the artists who design stamps have never done one honoring the post office?" He said, "I think they're afraid people will spit on the wrong side."

F-F Here's something else that bothers me: Why is it that the post office has stamps of famous people like Marilyn Monroe, Martin Luther King—what I want to know is where's the commemorative series celebrating Charles Manson?

C-C And another thing, stamps only depict old-fashioned inventions like the steam engine or the phonograph. What about the important modern inventions, like the breast implant?

D-D They could release them in pairs.

F-F Hey, I'd be a collector.

B-B Of course, guys would lick them on both sides.

That was tough, but it's typical. There's only one joke that's an A-A, a couple of Bs, and a few Cs. Admittedly I'm a hard rater, but I was surprised that some of the jokes didn't get a better response. It's actually kind of embarrassing to publish my failures, but how else can I teach you that joke writing has a rather low rate of success?

As much as I'd like to talk myself out of it, I'm only going to keep the jokes that have an A, B, or C rating. Some of the Ds and Fs are my favorite jokes, but I'm not going on stage merely to amuse myself. I want the audience to laugh.

Edit, Rewrite, and Rearrange

I put these three together because they often overlap. For example, when you edit something, you often have to rewrite other jokes, which leads to rearranging the whole routine. When you rewrite one joke, you usually have to edit others and then rearrange the routine. If you rearrange the routine, you'll have to rewrite . . . I think you get the idea.

Editing the Jokes

The ability to ruthlessly edit your own jokes is the most valuable skill you'll ever learn in comedy. Most funny people hold onto their jokes as if they were their children. They keep them whether they're good or bad. The sooner you're willing to cut out the marginal jokes, the sooner your show will move up to a professional level.

If a joke continues to miss, take it out of your show and put it aside. Notice I didn't suggest you throw it away. If you thought there was something funny there (and obviously you did since you went through the trouble of writing a joke about it), there probably is. Put the joke or routine aside for a while and let it percolate through your unconscious until something tells you to pull it out again.

Comics have put aside jokes and routines they could never get to work for years, only to finally pull them out again and find they've become killer bits. What changed? Maybe the comic's style of delivery or their persona; maybe he or she learned more craft and now possesses some new skill that makes the joke work. So remember to save those old bits you take out of your show. Eventually you may salvage a joke, a premise, or even an entire routine.

Here are the jokes I'm going to edit out of my post office routine because they didn't get enough laughter or any laughter at all:

D-D First of all, the post office has the audacity to have the logo of an eagle streaking through the sky. Yeah, right. It should be something more like a slug taking a nap.

D-D It frustrates me because the post office is a monopoly. If it had to operate like a real business, it'd be about as successful as a steak house in India.

C-D Just the term *postal service* is an oxymoron.

F-F I'd been in line for about ten minutes and it's getting even longer, so I yelled, "The line is getting longer, can you please close one of the windows." They did.

D-C To change the subject a little bit, I asked him, "Why is it that the artists who design stamps have never done one honoring the post office?" He said, "I think they're afraid people will spit on the wrong side."

F-F Here's something else that bothers me: Why is it that the post office has stamps of famous people like Marilyn Monroe, Martin Luther King—what I want to know is where's the commemorative series celebrating Charles Manson?

And one of the tags for the last joke about breast implants.

F-F   Hey, I'd be a collector.

Rewriting the Jokes

I use the term *rewriting* to refer to reworking or rephrasing jokes. For working on a routine, I use the term *rearranging*. They're discussed separately here, but in practice these tasks go hand in hand. When you rewrite a joke you'll need to rearrange the routine, and when you rearrange the routine you'll need to rewrite some of the jokes so they'll make sense within the context of the new routine.

When a joke doesn't work it's not always as simple as, "It didn't get a laugh, so take it out." Before editing the joke out of your show, try to figure out why it didn't work. It's amazing how much information you can pick up about a joke just by performing it. If you have an intuition about the joke or feel confident it can be salvaged, then play around with it to see if you can make it funnier. Here are some suggestions:

MAKE SURE THE JOKE WAS HEARD CLEARLY
Play back the joke to find out if you bobbled a word or unintentionally mumbled something. You'd be surprised how often that happens. The audience can't laugh at a joke they don't hear.

REFER TO THE GUIDELINES IN "CHAPTER 4, FROM FUNNY TO FUNNIER"
Ask yourself questions relating to the techniques discussed in this chapter for each joke that didn't hit the mark. Is the joke concise? Is the reveal at the end of the punch? Is there an obscure reference? Can the joke be improved with a hard consonant word? Might it work better by acting out the POVs? If you find that a guideline applies, use it in rewriting the joke.

PUT THE JOKE ON THE JOKE DIAGRAM
Another approach is to analyze the joke on the Joke Diagram. Ask questions relevant to the different aspects of the joke's structure. Do all the parts of the joke function well? Does the setup create a specific target assumption? Do you have a clear connector? Is the reinterpretation a surprise? Does the punch completely reveal the 2nd story? Is there another situation/story that will better express the reinterpretation?

Here are the remaining jokes from my routine. The parts that I've rewritten are underlined. I rewrote the following joke because I think it's a very funny idea, and I know I can get a better response with it:

C-C The other day, I was standing in line and I was checking out one of those mug shots of this particularly tough, nasty looking lowlife—it was the employee of the month.

Whenever a joke has such a strong target assumption, connector, and reinterpretation and still doesn't get the laugh it deserves, I assume that what's lacking is my ability to articulate. Here's the rewritten version:

I was standing in line looking at a seedy-looking picture of a . . . what do you call 'em? [I'm baiting someone in the audience into saying: "Mug shot" or "criminal" or "wanted poster," so I can say:] No, employee of the month.

These next four jokes received a very good response, so let's not fix what isn't broken.

C-B Maybe I'm being too tough on postal workers. After all, they are actually very efficient—with guns.
C-B Hey, their motto is: "Neither snow, nor rain, nor gloom of night shall keep them from their *rounds.*"
B-C And the thing that gets me, I don't understand why so many postal workers kill other postal workers. You'd think they'd be killed by disgruntled customers.
A-A After hearing me trash the post office, a postal worker said to me, "You shouldn't insult postal workers." I said, "Why not?" He said, "Because we know where you live."

This joke got a weaker response than the previous joke that it tags:

C-A I said, "Even if you did come after me, you'd show up at the wrong house."

Here's how I rewrote it. If this version doesn't get a better response, I can always pull it out or use the original.

Just don't hire a hit man because you'd send him to the wrong house.

This next joke worked okay but it needed an introduction because the original one was part of the Charles Manson joke that I edited out of the routine.

C-C And another thing, stamps only depict old-fashioned inventions, like the steam engine or the phonograph. What about the important modern inventions, like the breast implant?

So I simply lifted the introduction from the Manson joke and stuck it onto the front of this one.

Here's something else that bothers me, why is it that the post office has stamps that only depict old-fashioned inventions, like the steam engine or the phonograph. What about the important modern inventions, like the breast implant?

This joke, a tag of the previous joke, should have gotten a better response.

D-D They could release them in pairs.

So I rewrote it this way:

They could be the first stamps sold as a pair.

The tag below got a good response, but I know that after performing it several times, I'll figure out just the right rhythm that will pop a bigger laugh.

B-B Of course, guys would lick both sides.

Rewriting isn't an exact science. It involves as much trial and error as the initial writing. The one luxury is that if your rewrite makes the jokes worse, you can always go back or try another version.

Rearranging the Routine

There are many reasons for rearranging the jokes within a routine and the routines within a show. For instance, as you write new material and improve old jokes and routines, the bits that rank as your A material may become your B material and you'll need to change the order of your show. Or you may want to insert new jokes into established routines. To work the new material in, you'll probably have to rearrange parts of the routine.

Some say that an audience makes a decision about whether or not you're funny within the first thirty seconds. That decision can affect the rest of your show and be very tough for you to alter. That's why it's important to open with a strong bit. However, the audience tends to remember and judge you by your last few minutes on stage. Some people consider that part of the show to be even more important than the opening. That's why comics generally arrange their shows to close with their best bit. The following tools can help you rearrange your show.

Learning Your B, C, As
Having gone through the A, B, Cs of comedy, you're now going to learn the B, C, As. A comedy rule of thumb is to open your show with your second-strongest or B material, put your weakest stuff or C material in the middle, and close with your best or A material. Hence, the routine or show should be ordered B, C, A.

This makes a lot of sense, because if you open with your C material you may lose the audience, but you don't want to give them your A material first, either. Then you'd have nothing stronger to follow it with, and the show would end with a thud. If you get the audience laughing with your B material, however, it'll make the C material work even better. Then you can top yourself and close with your A material.

Graphing Your Show
Graphing is a great technique for plotting the overall effectiveness of your show. As you listen to the play-back of your show, rate the jokes from least funny to the funniest, and place dots for each rating on a piece of paper to form a graph. This isn't Comedy Lab 101, so it doesn't have to be perfect. It's just a simple method of seeing how your show climbs and falls.

If your show graphs like this on Diagram 13:

Diagram 13

```
              *          *
         *         *          *
     *       *                      *
  *
```

You have a problem with the pacing because it's funnier in the middle. You'll want to rearrange the jokes so the show ends with the jokes that get the biggest laughs.

This is what your show's graph should look like on Diagram 14:

Diagram 14

```
                                        *

                              *
                         *
               *      *
          *
    *      *
```

This kind of show builds steadily upward; some jokes may get an equal response, but none should get significantly less laughter than the jokes that came before it. The show should continue to get bigger and bigger laughs, ending with the biggest laugh of all.

HAMMOCKING
Hammocking refers to a technique of hanging weaker or riskier material between tried and true jokes or routines. There are several reasons to employ hammocking.

- *When you're trying out new material*, the jokes have a better chance of getting a good response if you already have the audience laughing. And if the new material totally bombs, the strong material that follows will bring your show back up.
- *When you want to practice riffing*, pick a time to do so between strong bits. This keeps you strong going in and strong coming out. If your riffing takes a nose dive, you can pick it back up. If you're doing well, just continue riffing. Remember, your job is to be funny, not just do your show.
- *When you're filling the time.* For example, if you only have twenty-five minutes worth of material and you book a forty-five minute gig, you'll be throwing in everything you've ever thought of. Stretching yourself like this is very good for you as an artist, but it's stressful. One way to maximize your material is to hammock the uncertain bits so they're surrounded by routines that consistently get laughs.

END WITH THE SEX MATERIAL

Here's something else worth considering when you're structuring your show: People tend to laugh harder at sexual material than they do at nonsexual material. Since that's the case, it follows that you should end your show with sex jokes. To test this theory out, rent any of Richard Pryor's concert videos. He always ends with dick jokes. Watch Jay Leno's monologues on *The Tonight Show*. Nine times out of ten he closes on a big laugh from a joke with sexual subject matter.

This doesn't mean that you should end your show with raunchy material. Sex jokes can be playful without being crass. But whether it's playful or raunchy—end your show with the sex jokes.

PLACE THE MORE CONTROVERSIAL BITS NEAR OR AT THE END OF YOUR SHOW

Controversial material often works better after you've gained acceptance with the audience. A routine that could alienate the crowd if you opened with it may work just fine once you and the audience have become friends.

With these guidelines in mind, I rearranged what was left of my jokes into a routine. As I looked the jokes over, it occurred to me that a little story line had developed in which I'm at the post office and end up having a conflict with one of the postal workers.

To have this story line make sense I had to find a reason for being at the post office. Then the other jokes could be things that happened while I was there. That meant that I had to write a new introduction to the routine. Here's what I ended up with:

> Yesterday, I went to the post office to get some stamps. I'm standing in a very long line that disappears over the curve of the earth. To amuse myself, I start thinking that the post office only offers stamps with old-fashioned inventions on them, like the steam engine or the phonograph. Hey, what about the important modern inventions, like the breast implant? They could be the first stamps sold as a pair. Of course, guys would lick both sides. Next, I notice on the wall a seedy looking picture of a . . . what do you call 'em? [I'm baiting someone in the audience into saying: "Mug shot" or "criminal" or "wanted poster," so I can say:] No, no, employee of

the month. Maybe I'm being too tough on postal workers. After all, they are actually very efficient—with guns. Hey, their motto is "Neither snow, nor rain, nor gloom of night shall keep them from their *rounds*." And the thing that gets me, I don't understand why so many postal workers kill other postal workers. You'd think they'd be killed by disgruntled customers. After hearing me trash the post office, a postal worker says to me, "You shouldn't insult postal workers." I say, "Why not?" He says, "Because we know where you live." I say, "Just don't hire a hit man because you'd send him to the wrong house."

Since the "we know where you live" joke has the highest rating, I decided to use that to close. There it is. This routine still needs more polishing, but it's getting there.

Of course, you can only do so much speculating at home. The only real means of evaluating a show is by performing it.

Rehearse and Perform Again

I include this to reinforce the idea that polishing a show is a loop. Now that I have a new version of my show, I'll reenact it in the Rehearsal Process, then go to a nightclub and perform it a couple of times. Then, I'll play it back and polish it all over again.

Get out into the clubs and perform as often as possible. The more you perform, the better you'll become, and the more feedback you'll get about what works and what doesn't.

At first you'll need to edit, rewrite, and rearrange after every show or two. As you perform your show more often, it'll require fewer radical changes. And soon you'll polish your delivery, know how to get a big laugh with every single joke, and shine like a professional.

Glossary
of Comedy Nomenclature

1st Story   The scenario imagined in the mind of the audience based on the setup of a joke.

2nd Story   The scenario imagined in the mind of the audience based on the punch of a joke.

Ad-Lib   To make up a joke within a scripted show.

Assumption   1. The audience's expectation that the 1st story will continue along the predicted line of thought. 2. Everything one is not experiencing with one's senses in the present moment.

Beat, Take a   A pause; to take a break for the purposes of comic timing.

Bit   A section of a stand-up comedy show or routine; also a short routine or a section of a routine.

Blue Material   Jokes using graphic sexual overtones, scatological (toilet) references, and swear words.

Bomb   To perform a comedy show which gets no or few laughs.

Booker   A person who hires and/or pays comedians to work in nightclubs.

Callback   A joke that refers back to another joke performed earlier in the show; often presented in a different context.

Capper   An antiquated term for the final in a series of jokes on the same subject matter which ends the routine with the biggest laugh.

Catch Phrase   A common phrase said in an extraordinary manner, which becomes the trademark of a particular comedian. For instance, Steve Martin's "Excuse me" or Billy Crystal's "You look marvelous."

Character POV   The perceptual position achieved when pretending to be someone or something else.

Closing Line   The final joke of a stand-up comedy show that normally gets a huge laugh.

Comedian Someone who makes his or her living being funny by means of an amusing character.

Comic Someone who makes his or her living being funny by telling jokes.

Connector At the center of a joke, the one thing interpreted in at least two ways. One way of interpreting it constitutes the target assumption; the second way of interpreting it reveals the reinterpretation.

Critic Spot A location designated for evaluating one's show; separate from the Rehearsal Space.

Flop Sweat The overabundance of perspiration one experiences from a panic reaction to bombing.

Flopping Bombing; not getting laughs.

Gag File A joke file.

Gag A joke.

Gig A show business job.

Graphing A scaling device with dots on paper for evaluating the effectiveness of jokes to determine their proper placement within a routine or show.

Hack From the British word *hackneyed*. Overused and thus cheapened; trite.

Hammocking A technique for placing weaker material or improvisation between two strong comedy bits.

Headliner The third and last comedian considered the star of a standard stand-up comedy show.

Heckler An audience member who talks and interrupts a show, usually by exchanging insults with the comedian.

Improvisation Akin to ad-lib, but usually refers to the spontaneous making up an entire bit or the continual comedic conversing with audience members.

Inside Joke A joke referring to information only a select group of people have.

Joke A device for expressing humor that employs a setup which contains a target assumption to misdirect the audience into accepting a bogus 1st story; and a punch which contains a reinterpretation which creates a 2nd story that shatters the target assumption.

Joke Diagram A visual aid for illustrating the structure of a joke.

Joke File Jokes organized and stored on index cards or in a computer.

Joke Map   The first part of Joke Prospector Writing System, which starts with a topic, creates a punch–premise, forms a setup–premise, and concludes with writing joke setups.

Joke Mine   The second part of the Joke Prospector Writing System, begins with a setup and explains the process of using the joke mechanisms of target assumption, connector, and reinterpretation to write a punch.

Joke Prospector   A joke writing system consisting of two parts: the Joke Map and the Joke Mine.

Jokey   1. A term used to describe such obvious jokes that one would expect to hear a rim shot following them. 2. A comic's groupie.

Kill   To give an excellent comedy performance.

Laughs Per Minute (LPM)   A measurement for counting the number of laughs in a show.

Lineup   A list of the comics slated to perform.

M.C.   Master or Mistress of Ceremonies; the person who introduces the performers.

Middle   The second comedian in the standard three comedian stand-up comedy show lineup.

Mike   Abbreviation for microphone.

Monologue   A speech for one person; in comedy, a stand-up comedy script for a solo comedian.

Narrator POV   The perceptual position achieved when being an observer or nonparticipant of an experience.

Neuro-Linguistic Programming (NLP)   A behavioral model and set of explicit skills and techniques founded by John Grinder and Richard Bandler. Defined as the study and mapping of the structure of the mind.

On the Road   Continually working outside of one's city of residence.

One-Liner   A joke made up of only one or two sentences.

One-Nighter   A job that only lasts one night.

Open-Mike   A policy to allow anyone to get on stage and try to be funny.

Opener   The first of three comedians in a standard comedy club lineup.

Opening Line   The first joke of a stand-up comedy routine.

Pause   To stop talking in a show to enhance the timing of a joke.

POV   Point of view.

Premise   The central concept from which a series of jokes or a routine is written.

Punch   The second part of a joke that contains a reinterpretation that creates a 2nd story that shatters the setup's target assumption.

Punch Line   Same as punch.

Punch–Premise   A step in the Joke Map stating a negative opinion about a smaller aspect of the topic.

Regulars   Comedians who appear frequently at a particular nightclub.

Rehearsal Space   A location designated for evaluating one's show; separate from the Critic Spot.

Reinterpretation   The mechanism in the punch that reveals an unexpected interpretation of the connector that shatters the target assumption.

Reinterpretations   Several alternative interpretations of the connector, other than the target assumption.

Reveal   Within the punch, the pivotal word, phrase, or action that exposes the 2nd story's reinterpretation.

Riffing   Verbally bantering with the audience.

Rip into or **Ripping**   To attack, insult, or verbally tear into an audience member or comic who has heckled or otherwise deserves the abuse.

Roll, On a   Delivering a string of jokes so that the audience continues laughing for an extended period without interruption.

Routine   Jokes all on the same subject or story that can be repeated on a regular basis.

Running Gag   Multiple callbacks; a recurring joke within the same show.

Schtick   A Hebrew word meaning a comic scene or piece of business; often implying physical comedy.

Segue   A transitional sentence for purposes of leading from one joke or routine to another.

Self POV   The perceptual position achieved when performing as one's self while participating in an experience.

Set   A stand-up comedy show of any length.

Setup   The first part of a joke that contains a target assumption to misdirect the audience into accepting a bogus 1st story.

Setup–Premise   A step in the Joke Map stating the opposite opinion to that of the punch–premise from which setups are written.

Shatter   With reference to joke structure, the point at which the audience realized that their assumption is incorrect.

Showcase   To perform a stand-up comedy show for little or no compensation for the purposes of getting experience or being seen by a potential employer.

Showcase Club   A comedy club using a lineup of ten or more comics in a row.

Sight Gag   A physical joke meant to be watched.

Stage Time   The duration, in minutes, a comedian spends in front of an audience making them laugh.

Tag or **Tag Line**   An additional punch immediately following a punch that does not require a new setup.

Take   A comedic facial reaction. Like the long Jack Benny take to the audience.

Target   A shorter term for target assumption.

Target Assumption   The misdirecting assumption in a joke's setup, which creates the 1st story and is shattered by the reinterpretation.

Throw Away   To put little emphasis on a point usually considered important.

Time Slot   The specific spot a comedian occupies within a showcase club lineup.

Timing   The use of tempo, rhythm, pause, and so on to enhance a joke or tailor it to an individual performing situation.

Topic   The single and overall subject of a routine based on a problem.

Topical   Jokes about current events.

Topper   An antiquated term referring to a joke playing off a previous joke; same as tag.